Dedicated to the salespeople of the business world,
the only true "Indispensables."
Without you nothing else happens...

Contents

SECTION 1

A hero is no braver than an ordinary man. He is just braver 5 minutes longer.

RALPH WALDO EMMERSON

Introduction

The dentist, heights, public speaking, snakes ... cold calling

Waiting at the dentist recently I picked up a magazine for young men. I can't remember which one. Anyway, flicking through the pages I found an instructional article with a title something like: "How to date young women." Buried in the inevitable survey accompanying this research was an interesting statistic—apparently the biggest fear afflicting young men who are active on the dating scene, is the very first approach.

It doesn't require a genius to get to the bottom of this fear: the anticipated rejection, humiliation, cruel laughter of friends, cumulative damage to self-confidence and ... er ... all that.

This *first-step-fear* is deeply ingrained. It is, apparently, felt by 99% of young men in just about every global culture in which free selection of a mate is allowed. The basic drive to find a mate is strong and primeval. The need to find a suitable woman and then attract her requires the knack of selling oneself. Selling the image of protector, lover, provider, and macho-man can only be done once the initial hurdle has been cleared—and this is the problem.

We all want to be Rambo ... but not in any dangerous or embarrassing situations

Selling anything to anyone (even yourself to somebody else) requires a first step. It is the mental projecting-forward of what could possibly happen when this first step is taken that, for most sales people, sets off the loudest internal alarm bell. "Put me across the table from a prospect," they say, "and just watch me sell ... face-to-face I'm untouchable! But please don't ask me to make a cold call. Why? ... well anything could happen!"

As a veteran sales person, trained by Rank Xerox in London over 35 years ago, then molded by Grand Metropolitan Hotels in the UK, and finally honed by global news and financial giant Reuters in Europe, Asia, and the US, I am here to offer you a real, practical, solution.

For the first time in any sales book, I am going to show you how, without running away from the fear, or indulging in endless bouts of positive thinking, or sitting crossed legged in a meditative corner serenely saying *"Ommm"* to yourself, you can cold call well and remain as chicken-hearted as you're secretly inclined to be.

At this stage if you're reading this in a bookshop in Europe, US or Asia you may still be inclined to put this back on the shelf and walk away believing there is another way. But please stop for one moment. There is something important you need to be aware of:

> **Fact:** In any market **85%** of the available new business goes to the **5%** of sales people who know the secret of successful cold calling.

If that doesn't convince you that's OK—you can now put the book back on the shelf and remain one of the average 95%. However, if you are really serious about being seriously successful, then read on. The tools for achieving everything you have ever wanted are in these pages.

So what are you going to find out?

Well if you're a "numbers game" cold caller whose job entails selling windows, or cheaper utilities, or telephone services to random, irritated householders just as they are trying to get the kids to bed, there isn't much here for you. I've never done it and it appears to be a terribly difficult job. That type of "telephone directory" calling allows you very little scope for the researched and planned contact, which is far more lucrative and much easier. In these pages you are going to discover an effective and simple way to make satisfactory first contact with brand new "business" customers for your business—and you're going to do that in six sections.

Here in the first section I want to make sure that we understand each other by setting down, in black and white, that this book is not about how to get rid of butterflies, fear, and cowardice. Indeed, I am going to show you how to use your fears to make you one of the best telephone sales people you know. In order to do this, I am going to introduce you to some very effective manipulative psychology, which you can use on that thing between your own ears: your brain. Until you've worked out how to get your brain thinking properly, all the selling tools, skills, and knowledge I can offer you, count for nothing.

> **"There is nothing either good or bad but thinking makes it so."**
>
> HAMLET

In Section 2—**Marking out the chicken run**, we are going to make sure that you fully understand why "selling" (of which cold calling is only one part), is the most important activity for your business. I cannot over emphasize this point, and I will even go further and state that it is not just a matter of *my* opinion. Ask any successful entrepreneur or top business executive and they will also tell you that there is simply nothing more important than selling for any commercial enterprise. This remains the case, even if you believe that selling is something that you, personally, are really too busy to do. One owner of a failing business I was called in to help two years ago, referred to his salesforce as "a bunch of necessary *yobbos*"; he just didn't get it – and yes, his business failed.

We will also consider what works best at each stage of the sales process and how to analyze and present yourself and your product. I will show you exactly how to convince the person on the receiving end of your cold call, that you are a person worth listening to.

If you speak too fast, or too slow, or your voice is too flat, or too slick, you will switch the other person's brain off in less than 30 seconds. In addition to all that, if you break the law by, making a sales call to someone listed on a preference service operated by the telephone authorities in a particular country (including the UK, US, Canada, Australia, and many others), you will not only switch them off but will also be liable to a substantial fine (if, that is, you haven't done the necessary research and checked them out first).

Once you've read through the first two stages you will be ready for Section 3—**The big secret of successful chickens.** Here I'm going to let you in on the ultimate secret of success, not only relevant to cold calling but also in the military forces, medicine, law … in fact, in every area of life you can think of. In this book I will show you exactly how to develop and use this secret to get everything you desire. Notice that I didn't say "anything" you want, which means "any one thing." I said *everything* in your life you truly desire. It doesn't matter whether you believe it or not because the method I will show you works for everyone who adopts it. As the Nike company strapline says "Just do it."

Section 4—**Being a persuasive chicken** demonstrates why it is almost impossible to persuade other people by "telling" them anything about your product or service. Customers (and we're all "customers") make most buying decisions emotionally. Only when the emotions are satisfied do we justify buying decisions with "facts." So what can you do about that when you are the seller? Quite a lot when you substitute your usual product statements for the right conversational questions. You will also see why the classic, "phone-pitch-mistakes," made by average cold callers, actually generate sales objections. It is not hard to get this right, it is just a habit you need to nurture. You need to be very clear on this because, as I said before and despite all you may believe, we rarely persuade any other human to do anything by "telling" them to do it. Whether it's a young man trying to attract a young woman, or you trying to persuade your prospective customer to see you or buy from you, the gift of the gab is not persuasive. The point is you never persuade other people to do anything … people persuade themselves.

Section 6—**How to keep them delivering the golden eggs** is one of the most important parts of this book when considering the growth of your business. This is because most businesses, just like yours, spend a fortune seeking new customers. Meanwhile, these average organizations treat their existing customers as the business equivalent of a "one-night-stand."

> Executives in these "average" businesses fail to understand that the biggest reason their existing customers drift away is that they simply forget about them.

All the available research shows that it is 90% easier and less expensive to get more business from an existing satisfied customer than to go out and find a new one. As a cold calling chicken you really need to do the many, easy, things described in this section if you want to keep the number of cold calls you make to the absolute minimum!

Oh and one last point ...

As you read through this book I'd like you to remember one thing: I am not *better* than you. I am just as naturally disinclined towards cold calling as you are, and I get my share of rejection and rudeness too.

So, I am not asking you to do anything that I don't do or have not verified myself. This is a book about practical things you can do today. I personally use all the techniques in this book to help find new customers for my business and to tear the heart out of most of my competitors. Most of my competitors are sitting there, complacent, self-satisfied, and with their eye off the ball—"*Cold call? Us? Moi?! ... Not necessary. Our clients always come back to us when they need to!*" Don't be too sure guys ... I am steadily stealing your top clients from you. And, dear reader—in your market area, so can you.

The real reason my competitors—and yours—don't cold call is very simple. They're too chicken to! In fact, a few years ago I made a terrific discovery on this subject. It was quite simply, that 95% of humans (including most people who need to cold call) are walking through their lives playing a continuous cassette tape in their heads. The message on the tape isn't great and it doesn't help at all. It is probably the same one that's playing in your head. Let me take a guess at what it's saying to you:

"What will people do when they discover I'm only me?"

If that's the case you've chosen the right book. So start to turn the pages and enjoy the ride.

SECTION 2

The elevator to success is out of order. You'll have to use the stairs, one step at a time.

JOE GIRARD – WORLD'S GREATEST SALESMAN
(GUINNESS BOOK OF WORLD RECORDS)

Marking out the chicken run

"Whether you think you can …
or you think you cannot …
… you're absolutely right"

HENRY FORD
THE FOUNDER OF FORD MOTOR COMPANY

Cold calling is simply the first stage of the selling process and I'd like to talk to you about exactly what that word "selling" really means. For a start, has anybody ever convinced you to buy something that you knew full well you would never use? How did they do it? Did you ever buy anything else from them? Did you subsequently have a good relationship with them? These are some of the questions that come up when you think about what types of sales techniques you should adopt.

My initial sales training was way back in the early 1970s. It was, looking back, very confrontational. It was full of manipulative tricks and "clever Dick" answers. For example, when cold calling a potential customer for the first time, the first person we might talk to would be the switchboard operator, secretary, or personal assistant to the person we actually wanted—these days we often hear these people described as "gatekeepers." We were trained to be very dismissive of gatekeepers. If a so-called gatekeeper asked us why we wanted to speak to their boss we were told not to get involved in a discussion but to say: "It's a business matter I need to talk to him (her) about. Would you put me through, please!" very nasty.

The chances of getting away with that today are practically zero. This approach led to the perfection and proliferation of sales techniques that focused not on the customer's needs or building a relationship—instead, they were about closing a sale. These methods often produced a one-time sale, which was all that many sales people were interested in.

By the time we got to the 1980s the recommended approach was softer and included key words like "ethics," "service," "relationships," "hard work," "quality," "delivery," and "loyalty." The training we were given then focused on building a friendship and relationship with each customer to make sure that they would keep coming back. By the end of the 1990s sales executives discovered that they could increase their sales by using certain words and researched persuasion methods. Most of these methods centered on the customer creating value in his or her own mind, by doing most of the talking instead of the sales person.

The basis of all these modern sales techniques, however different they may seem at first glance, was established in the 1950s on the A.I.D.A. principle (Attention, Interest, Desire, Action). This has been slightly modified over the years but remains essentially the same.

1. **Attention**: You have to get the attention of your prospect first, otherwise he or she will never begin to

listen to your proposition. The use of sensational headlines on the front of newspapers is the most obvious use of the attention-grabbing technique to initiate a purchase. Advertising companies receiving a brief from a client will spend the majority of their time thinking about the strapline. It is exactly the same in all forms of selling. Get the attention first.

2. **Interest**: Once you have the attention of the prospective customer you need to build his or her interest. Again, this is well illustrated by newspaper headline writers who use emotive words to gain the attention but omit the juicy detail. "POP STAR ARRESTED IN SEX SCANDAL" as a headline grabs *Attention* by using one of the four top most globally persuasive words: "SEX"* then peaks our *Interest* by not telling us who it is until we buy the newspaper. In face-to-face or telephone selling we get attention at the start by saying something which makes the prospect say or think: "What was that you said?" or, "Go on." The properly trained sales person will follow this with another sentence, very often a question, which further engages the attention without telling the whole story.

3. **Desire**: This is generated by the sales person helping the prospective customer to imagine and express the problem they have which the sales person knows he or she can solve. To illustrate this, trainers often tell the story of Socrates who was (allegedly) asked by a student: "Master, when will you tell me all I need to know?" Socrates took him down to the river and placed the student's head under the water. He kept him there until the student was fighting for breath. Even then he kept him down until he was desperate to get to the surface and just short of becoming unconscious. Only then did Socrates allow him to breathe. "You will know when you are ready for all the

---

*The other three most persuasive words in the English language are "win," "free," and "you."

knowledge you need, when your desire for the knowledge is as great as the need you had for breath just now. Until then I will keep you hungry for air." The well-trained sales person keeps the prospect as hungry for air as he or she can, by not giving away the solution until the customer is very aware of the problem they have and which the sales person's product can solve.

4. **Action:** Finally, the sales person has to encourage the prospect to act. "OK, well, thank you ... that was a very interesting proposition. We'll let you know soon," is still the sad and classic response at the end of an average cold call. The chances of ever hearing from that prospect again are slim. The sales person always needs to request some next action—agree the date for an appointment or even ask for the order. It is surprising how few do it.

Depending on the market there are many ways of "closing" a face-to-face or telephone sales call and it is worth outlining them here and expanding on them later:

- *A direct close or process advance*: Simply asking for the order or appointment when you are sure your prospect is ready. Offering a choice of two alternatives is often very useful here.
- *A deal/concession close*: Using this technique makes sure the prospective customer feels that he or she is making a good choice and saving money (or getting more value). It can be used with phrases like: "If you order today I can add this other module for only 10% more."
- *A scarcity close*: This one works well with statements like: "We only have two left but provided we agree now, then one of them is yours." A lot of sales people pull a face when they hear that—"It's old hat" they say. But walk down your local high street and you will see many examples of this everywhere: "Sale must end Friday!" The smart upmarket store where I buy my shirts has a permanent half price sale, in every branch, which ends every Friday

and re-starts every Monday! My favorite example is a store on Broadway in New York which for the past 20 years has had a sign in its window: "We are closing down. Everything must go!" When I started my training business a few years ago, I soon learned that keeping myself "rare" was a much more persuasive strategy than being immediately available, "tomorrow morning" for a new training job. Don't knock it. For a long time the diamond giant DeBeers kept diamonds (which were quite easy to find and numerous in the right locations) rare and valuable by carefully controlling their release into the market. Scarcity still sells; even planned scarcity.

- *Trial offer or "puppy dog" close*: You can also let the prospect use the product at no risk for a trial period. This works well if you're selling products that make people's lives easier. They aren't likely to want to give it back if it has saved them a lot of time and effort during the trial period. This often isn't as easy as it might appear because, for certain products, much work must be done in the trial period to encourage product use. If they haven't had the experience with the product you told them they would, then you probably won't get another chance.

So why did I tell you all this? Because believe it or not, as a sales person even a cold call chicken sales person, you are going to have to do *some* selling work and the broad steps you have to take have just been outlined above. But it's not a big issue because most of your competitors, like most of mine, are not working as hard at selling as they would have you believe.

> "Opportunity is missed by most people because it's dressed in overalls and looks like work."
>
> THOMAS EDISON

The powerful, 21st-century equivalent, method for cold call chickens which I have developed, and which I recommend to you is also explained in four steps. It is **I.K.E.A**. which stands for: Intelligence, Knock-on effect, Expansion, and Appropriate. Having the same initial letters as the well-known furniture store makes the I.K.E.A. approach easy to remember but why is it so effective? It is because it uses a very common sense approach to opening the sales process. This is based on the following three facts:

1. Most products and services are actually there to provide solutions to problems.
2. None of us is really a prospective customer for any product or service unless we have, first, admitted to ourselves that we have a problem that needs fixing.
3. As prospective customers, self-admission of a problem-in-need-of-a-fix depends largely on where we are on our own buying ladder.

The I.K.E.A. approach is based on first analyzing the potential problem-solving value of the product or service we wish to sell. Only when this is done can we begin to apply the I.K.E.A. model. So what does each word in the I.K.E.A. model stand for?

Intelligence

This is intelligence in the military sense. Rather than the usual random approach which is based on the old "it's a numbers game" philosophy ("The more people you call the more orders you get"—*yeah right! and the more rejections!*), use your head. Ask yourself who is out there who might have a problem your offering can fix? If you are not sure how your product fixes problems for existing individual customers simply go and ask them. If you are a completely new start-up company or have a new product in an existing company then sit down and ask yourself: "What problem are we trying to fix here?" Once you have established this, have a scan through the local and national newspapers, magazines, the Internet, and your existing client lists. Seek out similar companies and organizations that might just have the same problems you can potentially solve.

Another great source of potential business intelligence for you, is any newspaper, TV, radio or Internet news item concerning any type of big change affecting an individual company. When a company is going through any sort of traumatic change, new management, large-scale staff cuts, office closure etc., then opportunities in the area of new business abound for YOU! Any "big change" especially a change of management, generally foretells many smaller associated changes.

When new "senior managements" take over, they tend to initiate change in just about every area—cleaners, drinks machine vendors, stationery suppliers, computer repair people, recruitment consultants ... the lot.

Whenever I see such an announcement, especially one which includes the name of the senior person who is taking over or initiating the change, I call them. Always.

If a switchboard operator, PA or other gatekeeper tells me that their company is just undergoing a big change and there won't be any point in me talking to anyone any time soon, I know one thing: that person just doesn't know what's going on. They don't get it! Change is about to sweep through the place.

Old suppliers will be stripped out, being considered emblems of the "old philosophy," and new suppliers will be brought on board to represent the new wave. This is an especially advantageous time if your product or service offering is particularly visible to the lower orders of staff. The new boss will want people to both see and feel that it is different now and someone new is in charge. Yes it may be a power-game but from your point of view it's a great opportunity for some new business for YOU.

Knock-on effect

As with an iceberg, an admitted problem is usually only the tip of a much bigger issue lurking below the surface and affecting many aspects of the life of your prospective customer. The task here is to consider what possible knock-on effects there could be. Let's say, like me, that you're selling an executive sales training service. For a prospective customer, not meeting this year's sales target is not just a problem for the company's sales director. It will doubtless also affect cash flow, employee morale and retention, the employment prospects of many people, even the viability of the whole enterprise. By considering all the knock-on effects, you begin a powerful process, which will enable you to create value in the mind of your prospective customer when you eventually speak to them.

Expansion

With all the afore-mentioned information you can now expand the right message for the person you intend to cold call. For example, in the *Intelligence* step, you may have come across an announcement about a senior executive of a national company charged with leading expansion into the international marketplace. The expanded message for this person might be centered on the potential cultural, language, and unanticipated staffing problems which will be encountered in some countries when a foreign company sets up shop. (I chose this example specifically because it is based on a real life situation I successfully uncovered and cold called just a few months ago.) The objective of your message should be threefold:

1. Slightly disturbing—"What did you just say?"
2. Authoritative—your prospective customer gets the feeling that you know what you're talking about.
3. Based on value—as perceived by the potential customer.

Appropriate

Most initial sales approaches will only succeed if the cold caller has taken the time to analyze where the potential customer is on the buying ladder. If a potential customer has just bought a new copying machine he is already at the top of his current ladder and is probably not going to start a new climb—just yet. If, on the other hand, he has had an older copying machine for sometime, he will be at a lower point on a new ladder and will be more open to listening to the advantages of a new purchase. By listening to the way people react and by doing sufficient homework before you even pick up the telephone, you can mold an appropriate message for the person you are calling. We call each move up a prospect's buying ladder a "nextstep." A nextstep may be a product sale but it is more likely to be a first meeting, a product demonstration or a presentation based on previous meetings. Whatever it is, a cold caller must know which nextstep (call it a minimum objective if you like) he or she has in mind before the cold call commences. In this way, the sales process is subtly directed toward a successful outcome by the sales person.

As you can see, the age-old A.I.D.A. and the very up-to-date I.K.E.A. approaches have many similar attributes. We will refer to the I.K.E.A. steps in more depth later in this book. It may seem to you that most of this is just common sense and that most people, including your competitors, are probably doing this already. I promise you they are not!

Most sales people are doing almost nothing to generate new business apart from "hoping" for something to come up—they are "hooked on hopium." Indeed, despite getting this far in the book you may still be one of them. Let's have a quick talk about selling in general and its place in business.

Selling is omnipotent

In any commercial enterprise there is nothing more important than "selling." There is plenty of "product" out there in every market. Believe me, you don't have to think up a new product or service to succeed. The big shortage in the business world, is the lack of people willing to sell what's out there already. In your business, if you don't have sales you don't need managing directors, CEOs, COOs, accountants, engineers, designers, "flashy" offices, beautifully letter-headed paper, gold-edged business cards, full stock rooms or anything else. Because the only thing that confirms you have a business is this: *Do you have any customers?*

First kill the big lies

The biggest untruth in sales is the old saying: "design a better mousetrap and the world will beat a path to your door." In the 21st century it just doesn't happen. If you're working for a large company with a big advertising budget worth tens or hundreds of thousands, or even millions of dollars you can spend it on media ads and promotions of every description and achieve sales that way. However, it is horrendously expensive and is still very hit-and-miss. As the US department store giant John Wanamaker said: "Half the money I spend on advertising is wasted. Trouble is I don't know which half."

At the other end of the media scale, classified ads, sales letters, and glossy flyers are cheap alternatives, but as anyone who has tried them as their primary sales tool will tell you, they are generally not at all effective. That's why they're cheap.

And OK, I know you've got a friend of a friend out there who "started a business," uploaded the website and then the phone never stopped ringing from day one. That's what we call the lottery theory: you spend a bit of money on a website then sit back and watch the millions roll in ... except that they generally don't for the vast majority. A few years ago, when I was working in the US there was an advertising sign by the side of the road out to Kennedy Airport in New York. It was put up by one of the Wall Street companies selling financial management services. Its headline read:

> # Next weekend somebody is going to win the lottery*
>
> *(Just not you)

It precisely sums up the situation for most people and most businesses: you're not going to get much in the way of sales and success unless you work for it. The Internet is great, but you have to face the facts—it is just another market with tens of millions of other sites just like yours. If this is the heart of your sales strategy then you will have to spend a great deal of search-engine and "pay-per-click" money to get seen with no guarantee of sales.

The most effective way to initiate sales is to pick up the phone and do it yourself

So let us begin. First of all it would be a good idea to define what we mean by "cold calling":

Cold calling is, simply, making contact with strangers.

You can familiarize yourself with cold calling today if you want to. It's a proven fact that one attribute lucky people have is that they know more people, so waste no more time. Risk being thought an idiot and try this: *get into the habit of chatting to people in public places.* A few people will make it clear they don't want to talk (sometimes that's me too, I'm not always feeling sociable). But I've discovered that, 80% of the time if you ask other human beings something connected to themselves and their wellbeing they will tell you.

As Dale Carnegie suggests in his book *How to Win Friends and Influence People,* published over 70 years ago, if you want other people to like you don't tell them about "you." Ask them about themselves.

For scientific reasons, described in the insert below—**The six degrees of separation experiment**—it almost doesn't matter who you talk to at this stage, but do get chatting. Make it easy on your self at first ... after all, this book is entitled *Cold Calling for Chickens*... so I guess you won't find it that easy (just yet), but, if you can, get into the habit of smiling and "small-talking" with people. For example, you can do it in the line at the bank, supermarket, or post office. *"Oh where did you get that asparagus, it looks nice." "It's great to have a sunny day for a change isn't it?" "Can I help you with that parcel for a moment?"* Or perhaps to the person sitting next to you on the plane *"Are you on your way home?"* By the way, the latter is my best "opener" which has brought me at least 10 new business contacts during the past year—so who cares about the few terse replies!

The six degrees of separation experiment

An experiment was performed in America in 1967 by an American sociologist called Stanley Milgram. He came up with a way to test his theory that the world is much smaller than we think. He believed that, because the 200 million adults who live in America, with a bit of prompting, can each identify at least 250 people they know by their first name, there must be some very close links between nearly everybody in the country.

He randomly selected 10 people in the Midwest and got them to agree to send packages to someone they had never heard of living in Massachusetts. The senders were given the recipient's name, field of work, and an idea of where they lived. They were each instructed to send the package to a person they knew, on a first-name basis, who they thought was most likely, out of all their family, friends, colleagues, and acquaintances, to know the final recipient personally. That next recipient would do the same, and so on, until the package was personally delivered to its target.

Although everybody expected the chain to include at least a hundred links, it only took an average of between five and seven "hops" across the 200 million adults to get each package delivered. The findings were published in *Psychology Today* and gave rise to the phrase "six degrees of separation." The same experiment was repeated in the UK a few years ago, where the population is roughly 20% that of America. In this case the average number of hops was just 4.

Footnote: A lot of people discounted this work in the 1980s and 1990s because they said Stanley Miligram's original sample was too small. In 2001, Duncan Watts, a professor at Columbia University, continued his own earlier research into the "six degrees" theory and recreated the experiment on the Internet. He used an email message as the "package" that needed to be delivered, and surprisingly, after analyzing the data collected by 48,000 senders and 19 target recipients in 157 countries, Watts found that the average number of intermediaries was, indeed, still 6.

Cold calling is something that, at some time, every business has to do. Just as all our bodies are different in terms of build, weight, height, color of hair and eyes, sex, age, brain power, and so on, they all have to do roughly the same things to stay alive, grow, and multiply. In the same way businesses are different in terms of their market, profession, size, growth targets, cash flow, and experience yet they all have to do the same things to stay alive, grow, and multiply. Sooner, or hopefully (much) later they are also going to die (nothing lasts forever).

But if something isn't done regularly to maintain the pipeline of new prospective customers then the inevitable loss of some existing customers will eventually lead to the premature death of the organization. So if you ask me what sort of businesses need to "cold call" and make contact with strangers who could become new customers the answer is *all* businesses need to do it.

The biggest slow killer of large successful companies is *complacency* and *all talk, no action*. In many of the sales offices I have visited, and still visit, in the middle of the morning, you will find sales people sitting at their desks "doing stuff." This stuff seems to range from emails, to phone calls, to sales meetings, to chats, to writing letters, to writing reports, to eating. But what is not heard is the sound of selling. The sound of selling in the middle of the day should really be the sound of silence. To explain why this is the case I'd like to take you back over 30 years.

The next 30 seconds will change your entire life

I read these words in 1970 and they did change my life. The job-ad with this headline was placed in a London newspaper by copying machine company Rank Xerox; I applied. A few days later I received an envelope with a business card inside. Across the front of it was written: "Call me." The card was from a man who—for the sake of this book—we'll call Bruce Cantle.

It was an unusual interview invitation but I called, I went for the interview and got the job … that's all you need to know for now. Bruce was District Manager for Rank Xerox in Croydon, South London. What he and Xerox taught me changed my life. And it can change yours too if you choose to follow his advice. It works for everyone—you just need to do it.

Bruce was a tall, balding man in his thirties with a brilliant track record in sales. His appearance was deceptive because he looked and sounded like a tall priest. Once we "new-boys" had been through the Xerox basic training we were sent back to our branches in various support/learning roles until a sales territory became vacant.

Once you were appointed to a territory they expected the real work to start; the company culture was that they carried no passengers.

Step 1 in our training manual was "Get Organized." **Step 2** was "Start Cold Calling." As **Step 2** was clearly going to be tough and needed a certain amount of preparation time we all spent a long time on **Step 1**. Indeed, most of us were still on **Step 1** after several days. Bruce, being an "old pro" knew all this, and he also knew that the real reasons we were still on **Step 1** became weaker as the days wore on. He would watch the developing situation and suddenly take action.

At about 11am after three and a bit days of "get organized" had passed, he suddenly appeared on the sales floor. It was his natural gait to proceed at high speed. He also had a very upright walking style, which, rather like a swan, meant that his upper body remained very still while from the waist down he moved rapidly. He charged up to the nearest "trainee desk" (mine in this case) calling out some 30 feet before he arrived and in a somewhat surprised tone: "Bob! ...Bob! ... Why are you here?!" Feeling that an explanation was in order I blurted out the first thing that came into my head. "Well Bruce, I'm just finishing off preparing my calling sheet. Then I have to write this letter to that customer who's relocating. And after that I need to brush up on my script and then ..." At this point Bruce interrupted and the whole office went quiet ... they knew the fun routine that was about to take place.

"No, No, Bob," he said in his kindly, admonishing vicar's voice, "That's your f - - - ing about speech! ... you see Bob ... (kindly tone) you're a young man ... just starting out in commerce ... and you haven't yet realized something very important. Do you know what that is? ... you don't? ... let me tell you then, it's this: there-are-no-customers-in-the-office! ... but maybe you think there are ... shall we look together?"

At this point he shaded his eyes with one hand in the manner of "I see no ships" and with a frown on his face turned this way and that saying: "No not as far as I can see ... nothing ... not a single one!"

Then he ran to the window overlooking the high street below and shouted excitedly: "Oh look ... there they are ... walking about down there and sitting over there in those office blocks ... their pockets are bulging with money. Quick, pick up a phone and talk to them before somebody else does."

Everyone in the office had seen this routine before and there was the usual guffaw of laughter. While this was dying down he invited me into his office, shut the door and sketched out the diagram you will find on page 62 of this book.

Dumb executives mix with other dumb executives

"Selling is simple," he said, "it just isn't easy. On the other hand it's not as hard as many of your colleagues in this office would have you believe either. Your best bet for the life you want is not inside this office. It's out there where the money is."

He pointed outside to our office "kitchen area" and asked me if I knew what it was. I replied that it was, obviously, "the kitchen." "No, unfortunately, that's what you're supposed to think," he said, "I don't know why they put them in offices. In fact it is a cunningly disguised machine! In other offices it's sometimes called the 'water cooler' or the 'drinks machine' or the 'coffee shop.' But do you know what these things are really? … No? They are all devices for sucking the happiness out of an office! Because when two or three sales people are gathered near them, and even if, up to that point they been feeling perfectly happy, they start to say something along the lines of: 'Jeez I'm tired,' 'Yeah..I'm fed up with this,' 'Nobody's buying anything.,' 'The competition's got much better products than ours,' 'The management just doesn't understand,' 'This is a terrible time of year to try to sell anything,' 'Nobody sees sales people on a Monday [Tuesday, Wednesday, Thursday, Friday],' 'And don't forget it's June … a terrible month June [July, August, September, October, November, December, January, February, March, April or May].everybody knows that,' 'You know Bruce [The Boss]? … He's a complete idiot. He doesn't know a thing,' 'I'm seriously considering leaving … I've got a job interview next week,' 'I don't blame you … I'm thinking of leaving too.'"

Bruce was right. I've been in selling now for over 35 years and worked for a number of different companies before setting up my own business. And here's the amazing thing; I always managed to join all those companies at a time when (if you listened to the people who were ALWAYS in the office or hanging round the coffee machine) they were going through the worst time, with the worst management, the worst products, the worst customers, the worst commission plan, and at the worst time of year, ever, in the history of their business. Kitchen areas, water coolers and drinks machines in general have something about them that sucks at enthusiasm.

There's only one thing more contagious than enthusiasm: lack of it

When you're in the office and especially anywhere near one of the unhappiness generators (*You'll have to identify them for your office but I bet you can think of at least one*), it is easy to get infected and become part of the problem. So spend as little time in the office as you can.

> "The best antidote for despair is action."
>
> JOAN BAYEZ

The people who bring in the business are rarely in the office and if they are in the office they're on the phone. Get out where the money is … there are no customers in the office, or, as one lady in the audience echoed when I said that at a seminar I was addressing in Chicago: "Yeah … like there are no boyfriends in the apartment!"

> "The notorious US bank robber, Willie Sutton was once asked by the Police why he kept robbing banks. He replied 'Because that's where the money is.'"

Getting rid of the infected desk-percher

If your sales job is 100% telesales and you're always in the office here's a quick way to handle the inevitable moaners. (*This is also useful for those of you sellers who occasionally have to be in the office so do read on.*) When you bump into one of the "infected people" in the coffee area, or if they come and perch on the end of your desk with their coffee, all ready to start spreading the contagion, let them start their usual routine: "Oh God ... I'm exhausted. That new manager really makes me mad ... I mean it! ... I'm sick and tired of all this. The service we give is awful and you might as well not tell management. ... The new commission plan stinks ... you know that as well as I do. ... Nobody listens! I'm seriously considering leaving ... it's just ... ridiculous! ... ridiculous! ... I mean... I'm wasting my time ... we all are!"

Then, when the complainer finally runs out of steam, do this: smile, stand up, laugh as if they've just told you something hilarious and say: "Yes I know, that's GREAT isn't it! ... You know you make me laugh you really do. Well ... I must get on ... talk to you later!" Then turn away and get on with your work. Here's the really funny thing; that person won't come back to bother you again for several weeks. Do you know why? Because of something that experts discovered a few years ago: **misery loves company**. If a moaner comes up against another human who refuses to be infected the moaner will simply go away. Give it a go and let me know what happens.

So, I repeat, spend as little time in the office as possible and when you're there stay away from the kitchen or wherever it is people meet to have a bitch about their life. If you have to go to the office arrange to do your cold calling very early or very late in the day before infectors get in or after they've gone home (*more on timing later—this bit is still about building your Attitude*). Get yourself outside as soon as you can. Do your phoning from home if you want to. Or standing by the lake in a park (my personal favorite). In these days of cell phones there is hardly any limit to the places from which you can do your cold calling. For most sales people you really don't have to do it in the office.

On the wall of a very successful sales office I visited while I was living in the US was a large clock. Half the face was covered by a sheet of brown paper blocking from sight, all the numerals in the six-hour segment from 10am to 4pm. The sales director is a great friend of mine now and he had a rule that no sales person could be in the office unless he or she could see the hour hand of the clock.

Across the brown paper was written this legend: **"If you want to make your daily score stay out of the office between 10 and 4"** (And if you can't stay out of the office stay out of the kitchen.)

You can't save time—only spend it

So what about you? Do you manage your time ... or does it manage you? Many sales people, it seems to me, bounce from one crisis to another. I have actually come to the conclusion that they secretly enjoy fire-fighting a crisis. "Oh no!" they say, "Another urgent crisis! It means I don't have time to do the real selling work, especially the cold calling, which, of course, I love." (*Yeah, right!*) What they are actually doing is hoping for something "lucky" to magically happen. Some sales people I know do this every day. How do they survive? How can anybody hope to bring in the sales they want if they are generally to be found in the office, fiddling with emails, crises, and reports in the middle of the day?

In my seminars I often use the following illustration to really bang home the importance (*read: total life sustaining imperative*) of making time for real selling and cold calling activity, every day.

I say, "OK, time for a quiz" and pull out an old-fashioned pickle jar. It's a very large, wide-mouth affair and I put it on the table in front of me. Then I also produce about a dozen fist-sized potatoes and carefully place them, one at a time, into the jar. When the jar is filled to the top and no more potatoes will fit inside, I ask, "Is this jar full?" Everyone in the seminar yells, "Yes."

In true fairground, side-show manner I then say, "Really?" I then reach under the table and pull out a packet of unshelled peanuts. I dump some of the peanuts in and shake the jar causing the nuts to work themselves down into the spaces between the big potatoes. I then ask the group once more, "Is the jar full?"

By this time the class is on to me. "Probably not" one of them always answers.

"Good!" I say. Once again I reach under the table and bring out a bucket of uncooked kidney beans. I start dumping the kidney beans in the jar and they go into all of the spaces left between the potatoes and the peanuts. Once more I ask the question, "Is this jar full?"—"No!" the group shouts.

Once again I say, "Good." Then I grab a packet of fine sugar and begin to pour it in until the jar is filled to the brim. Then, after a suitable pause I look at the delegates and ask: "What is the point of this illustration?"

One smart Alec always jumps up and states confidently: "The point is, no matter how full your day is, if you try really hard you can always fit some more things in it!" "Actually no," I say, "that's not the point I am presenting to you. The truth this illustration teaches us is this: If you don't put the big potatoes in first, you'll never get them in at all."

So what are the "big potatoes" in your business life? I'm sure I don't have to tell you but cold calling/prospecting/contacting new clients, whatever you want to call it, is one of them. Remember to put these big potatoes in first, every day, or you'll never get them in at all. Then your customers, the ones who usually come back for more, will be vulnerable to people like me who WILL take them away from you. So, tonight, or in the morning, when you are reflecting on this short story, ask yourself this question: What are the "big potatoes" in my business life tomorrow? Then, put those in your jar first.

Time is the only thing that everybody on the planet has the same amount of every day. The main differentiator between sellers who succeed and those who are average or poor performers is how you use that identical allocation of time.

> **"None of us has enough time, but we all have all there is."**

There are some things that you can do to help yourself manage your time more effectively. Time management, for sales people, is a conscious decision. First of all, sales people—but especially you as a "cold call chicken"—need to *decide* what is important and then plan your selling day around these things. If you don't you'll find the day just fritters away on absolutely nothing. The key is to be proactive the day before. Don't hang about letting time make its demands on you—put yourself in the captain's chair and decide what you will do with tomorrow. What are your goals for the day? Where do you want to end up? What is truly important to you? What actions do you need to take to make those things happen? And if you only take one action make it the one described in the following story.

All the time in the World

I saw the old thief, Father Time
Come hirpling down the road
He had a sack upon his back
Lost minutes were his load
He opened it and showed to me
Not minutes, but a host
Of years, decades a century
Or more of minutes lost
"I want to buy a year," I said
"And I shall pay you well"
"If earth's mould were finest gold
To you I would not sell
For I have stolen years from kings
From Milton, Shakespear, Bach
How could you buy such precious things
Your common gold is trash"
He tied his sack and said "Farewell
Young man, I have got my fee"
For while I tried to make him sell
He stole an hour from me.

Anon

In the early 1900s the American banker Charles Schwab asked Ivy Lee, an early practitioner of public relations and work place efficiency, to help him manage his time more effectively. Lee spent a week with Schwab and his staff and during this period observed the way they all used their time. They had many projects on the go and each had its updated list of "to-do" things and connected activities. At the end of the week he is reported to have presented Schwab with a single key recommendation. Schwab thanked Lee and asked him what his fee would be. Lee replied, "Pay me nothing now but promise me that you and all your staff proceed by following my recommendation, to the letter for thirty days. One month from today pay me what you think my advice was worth." Schwab agreed and at the end of the month made out a check to Lee for $35,000. So what was the advice that was worth this huge sum in the early part of the 20th century? Quite simply this: *Write your daily 'to-do list' prioritizing your top six tasks but always do it the night before.*

Why the night before? Why not first thing in the morning or even as things come up during the day? It seems that doing it any time other than immediately before you go to sleep is not half, a quarter nor even a tenth as effective as doing it the night before. A brain surgeon friend of mine who is also a psychologist (I mix in exalted circles you see!) suggests that the "night-before list" is actually mulled over by your brain while you're asleep. Even when you're sleeping, your unconscious mind is filtering and assessing all the information it's had thrown at it in the previous 12 hours and even starts to process and find answers to some of the problems and challenges. The old adage that you should "sleep on it" appears to have some sound basis in fact after all. So, it's well worth getting your brain to do some easy work for you while you rest and be grateful that it hasn't cost you the $35K it cost Charles Schwab to find it out.

Writing your to-do list the night before, (as I have found being both a cold call chicken and naturally completely disorganized person) is an extremely profitable way of planning and achieving solid progress each day. The steps are these:

1. Before you go to sleep each night list the various to-do items you would like to get done tomorrow.
2. Prioritize the top six items on your list (see table below).
3. The next day examine the list and begin with task number 1.
4. Do the job represented by the first item on the list. Once it has been completed cross it off and move on to the second item.
5. Continue through the top 6 items you prioritized yesterday evening until they are completed. Then endeavor to complete as much of the rest of the list as you can.
6. Do not get sidetracked. The top 6 items are the ones you MUST complete to achieve your goals. Items after number 6 may not be completed.
7. In the evening remake a list for tomorrow in exactly the same way. Some items may be transferred from today's list and after prioritization may not get done tomorrow either. Makes one wonder if they were ever that important.

Realistically, all this time management advice is not an absolute panacea. Can you always play a proactive role? Of course not. Emergencies *do* come up; you *must* often respond to a deadline. But you can cut the number of these *reactive* surprises by thinking and planning in advance—by being *proactive*.

Even the time management tool outlined above will not work for everyone all the time. Instead, you need to decide what works best for you, as an individual, right now. Do you need to schedule better? To prioritize more effectively? Do you work more productively in the morning? Are you trying to complete an entire project at one time instead of breaking it into more manageable chunks? What will work for you ... now?

One way of analyzing and planning your day can be found by considering the boxes in the following table. During a day we can define most of our activities as either **Important** or **Urgent** or **Important but NOT urgent** or **Urgent but NOT important**.

Time prioritization table for cold call chickens

Important tasks (*The big potatoes*)	**Urgent tasks** (*The kidney beans*)
Cold calling—7:45am to 9:15am. Face-to-face selling—10am to 12:30pm and 1:30pm to 4pm Cold calling also 5:30 to 6:15pm Don't take cellphone calls or send texts during **important task** time. Switch it off!	Unexpected things—9:15 to 10am and 4pm to 5pm You can switch on your cell phone in **urgent task** time
Important but not urgent tasks (*The peanuts*)	**Urgent but not important tasks** (*The fine sugar*)
12:30pm to 1:30pm lunch (and maybe a little cold calling?) 5pm to 6:30pm reports, meetings, proposals, emails, discussions with boss. (Plus weekends if necessary for the occasional cold call—you'll be amazed who you can get hold of!)	No time allocated for these thieves of time: chatting to family and friends on the telephone, chatting in the kitchen round the drinks machine, 80% of emails and most text messages

The important work for cold call chickens is made up of all the vital things that have to go into the **Important** box. These are the big potatoes in the jar from the earlier seminar example. No matter what else happens, you have to find time every day to make these happen. (*By the way, if you're not going to be really committed to this you might as well chuck this book in the wastepaper basket—this is at the heart of the secret of your sales success, immense wealth and everything you ever wanted but if you can't see that ... well it's up to you*) For anyone involved in selling, the important items are to do with maximizing the number of contacts you make with customers and potential customers. So in this **Important** tasks box go the following: *cold calls* with people you have never spoken to before; *warm calls* with past customers and current customers who you haven't spoken to for a while and people who have inquired about doing business with you; and *face-to-face contacts* with people you have made appointments with. During core times for these activities you must devote yourself to these things to the exclusion of everything else. If you, like me, are a procrastinator who can always find the *peanuts, beans* and *sugar* quickly filling up the space apportioned to the all important potatoes here are a few things you can do to get yourself to make sure they are done.

1. Don't think too much about the task in advance.
2. Don't let not wanting to do it be an excuse for not doing it.
3. Tell yourself you'll make a final decision when you get there.
4. Just start for 10 minutes.
5. Imagine how you will feel at 5pm tonight if you haven't had the courage to do it.
6. Imagine how pleased you are going to feel at 5pm tonight when you have actually done it.

So just how many cold or warm calls need to be fitted into the **Important** part of your working day? *As a general rule to cover most types of business I work with, the majority of you* *reading this book should be planning on an absolute minimum of 10 calls every day or 50 every week.*

I know there will be some of you telling me right now that your particular job demands many more and in some cases that can be 70 or more each day. In some purely "telesales" offices your daily target may be well over 100. But I often ask sales people across a variety of different business cultures to level with me about their true level of cold calls. The numbers I get are usually between 0 and 5 *per week*!

My recommended number in the previous paragraph is not a target for you. It is the "absolute minimum" for any of us. The truth is, unless you are absolutely brilliant at cold calling (and as you're reading this book I guess you know you have some work to do), one cold call each day is not going to get you where you want to be.

I recently attended a seminar in London which was addressed by the man who founded one of the world's leading Sushi Bar chains. He told the audience that when he started up 10 years ago he became very discouraged by his failure to successfully cold call the landlords and potential financial backers whose cooperation he needed in order to succeed. In the end he discovered a miracle way to do it. Rather than trying to succeed at each call he made "6 rejections per day" his daily target. It was through this change of emphasis that his fortune began to turn. He had discovered a universal truth, which in your case and mine includes cold calling. That is, however bad you are at applying cold calling technique, if you simply persist you will discover that not *everyone* says "no." As every successful person has found, you do have to hear a lot more "no's" than "yes's" on your way to your life's dreams. So spend your daily important task time seeking many more no's if you really wish to succeed.

The **Important but not urgent** box (the peanuts) is the next order of priority. In this box go all the other things you have to do in sales: attending internal meetings (including sales meetings), writing proposals, writing emails and letters to customers, planning your diary and all the other stuff that needs to be done but must not be taking up "core selling time." For most sales executives these tasks should be performed at the beginning and end of the day, *not* right in the middle—and yes, sometimes even at weekends! Horror! But hey, there's no such thing as a "part time really successful person" so weekends and evenings count too. In sales we get paid what we're worth and not for working 9 to 5! (Well, you said you wanted to be successful!)

The **Urgent** box (the beans) is for handling the fire-fighting and crises that do occur. But you need to *control* your availability to handle them. If you want an excuse for not doing the important work then carry on letting the urgent items control you. In other words: answer your cellphone whenever it rings; be visible and available in the office all the time especially when your manager is looking for someone to delegate an emergency to; offer to deal with any work problem that comes up during the day from a broken coffee machine to getting someone in to fix a blocked toilet. Immediately drop everything to take a new user manual to a client across the other side of town ... I assure you that any of us can easily fill up a day with all this "urgent" stuff. As C. Northcote Parkinson said in his book *Parkinson's Law* back in the 1950s: **"Work expands to fill the time available for it's completion."** Actually you can't put definite activities in this box but they are the things that *must* be handled sometime during the day ... today! So in order to control them, set aside say half an hour three times a day at 9am, 1pm, and 5pm. Outside these times make a pledge with yourself to: answer no incoming calls on either landline or cellphone; be hidden away somewhere, out of sight of anyone especially your manager. YOU WILL BE AMAZED AT HOW MUCH TIME THIS LIBERATES FOR YOU!

And finally the **Urgent but not important** box (the sugar) that permeates every corner and can very soon fill the jar (your day) to the very brim, leaving no space for either the beans, or the peanuts or even the potatoes. The stuff in this box is the biggest time-thief of all. I saw once on the TV game show *Family Fortunes* the question: "What is the main item stolen from workplace offices?" It wasn't paper or pens or note pads or staples ... *it was private phone calls*! "No I won't bother to call my sister in Florida from home ... I'll do it from work ... it's free there!"

In addition to this, there is the sheer banality and endlessness of the calls. In my capacity as an independent sales trainer I often have the opportunity to sit in sales offices, anonymously, at a spare desk and listen to some of the aimless telephone conversations. They are never just short to the point ... they go on and on and on for half an hour at a time about nothing: *"Well we went to this new restaurant on Friday ... I had the shrimp and John had the steak, but he didn't really like the sauce ... so the manager said ... so I said ... then he said ... so we... then I ... then she ... so that was a ruined evening. Then on Saturday ... he went to play squash but when he got there. ..."* On and on and on ... and on. Then there's the: *"I'm just popping out for a coffee anyone want one?"* scenario ... *"Are you? Oh well, I'll come with you then because I just need to pop into the Post Office because I must just post this letter ... and I will do some errands while it's quiet."* The effect of wasting your day, my fellow cold calling chicken, on urgent but not important work is that it totally devastates any chance you have of achieving all you ever dreamed of. Stay as "chicken" as you want to be, but remember that when today is gone you can't get it back.

Action plan for your time

As there are no time management tools that will work for everyone, all of the time, some of the following tips may help you in your search for tools:

- Learn to say "no."
- When possible, delegate.
- Don't let paperwork or emails pile up.
- Ask yourself, "What is my objective or goal today?"
- Place your effectiveness first.
- Break each job into bite-sized pieces; don't procrastinate because it can't all be done at once.
- Identify your time wasters especially "urgent but not important" things ... and resolve to eliminate them.
- Add specific, limited, times to deal with urgent items into your schedule.
- Save your sanity by realizing that it is not possible to please all the people all the time!
- Make sure you understand the truth contained in the Pareto principle (see below).

The Pareto principle

In the late 19th-century, an Italian economist called Vilfredo Pareto noticed that 80% of the money and property was owned by 20% of the population. His equation, often referred to as the "80/20 rule" or the "Pareto principle" seems to run true for a lot of things: 20% of the people make 80% of the complaints; 20% of the top sales people bring in 80% of the sales; 80% of our time is spent on 20% of the problems.

To manage your time effectively, you need to identify and address those things that eat up the biggest chunks of your time. You need to know what they are, and you need to know how much value they provide to what you do. Have a look at your day-to-day routine with Pareto's 80/20 rule in mind and see what you find. Make sure in future that you spend your time where the pay-off warrants it!

Check-up

Are you managing time or is time managing you? A simple "yes" or "no" response will help you to decide.

1. I often need to respond to crises or put out fires.
2. I don't set time for planning ahead and sorting out priorities.
3. When I leave work "on time," I feel guilty because of what has been left undone.
4. I have trouble devoting the time and energy I would like to family and/or friends.
5. Even when I'm home I find it tough to stop thinking about what's happening at work.
6. I often find myself caught up in "busy-work" or little things.
7. I don't make sufficient time for activities that build my professional reputation.
8. Just keeping my head above water is about all I can hope for.
9. I have trouble finding a time management system that works well for me.
10. It's often the same few problems or people that take up a large chunk of my time.

Responding "yes" to one or two of these statements probably indicates *time management* difficulties. Make some time now and plan ahead.

Accounting for your time

Not worrying about wasting time during the selling day is nothing short of self-delusion. Most sellers love self-delusion.

They are secretly relying on making a fast buck! But becoming successful and wealthy is something that the vast majority of successful and wealthy sales people have done by working from hour to hour, from week to week and from month to month. Right now I'd like you to do a quick calculation to work out the cost of your own time.

I am going to be fair to you and assume that after 4 weeks paid vacation plus national holidays, you work a 47 week year. Each day you work from 8am to 6pm with an hour off for lunch (9 working hours), which adds up to 45 hours a week or 2256 hours each year.

So now, write down the amount of money you want to make in the next 12 months. (*In the next section of this book we will examine the importance of setting yourself challenging goals so make sure your financial target for the coming year is both realistic and challenging.*)

My annual income goal is $x.

Divide that number by the number of working-hours in your year.

12 month income goal $x \div 2256 = \$x$ every hour.

Weekly income goal = your hourly figure $\times 47$

But that is not the end of your calculation because, of course, we don't sell every minute of every hour of every week. Some work time, as shown in our earlier table, will inevitably be spent in ancillary activities, which are shown in the **Urgent** and **Important but not urgent** boxes. So it is necessary to differentiate between these other activities and the persuasive activities in the **Important** box; these, a significant percentage of which are cold calls, are the activities you actually get paid for.

Look back over your last 5 working days. How many hours and minutes did you truthfully spend endeavoring to get commitments from customers and prospective customers? Don't kid yourself—if they were just courtesy visits to existing customers they don't count.

The next thing to do is to divide your weekly goal by those hours of actual selling time.

Weekly $x ÷ x hours of real selling time = $x

This is your current and true hourly selling rate—don't worry if you are shocked by that number. When we calculate the hourly selling rate for most sales people it often comes out at $1000, $3000 or $5000 an hour. That is the sort of money earned by brain surgeons and top lawyers.

It should encourage you not to waste another single minute of the time allocated to activities in your **Important** box. Especially, in the case of this book, the minimum two hours each day spent cold calling! Each of those daily persuading-hours is valued at between $1000 and $5000. Don't be fooled by all the urgent paperwork, emails, meetings and discussions and other routine stuff; it is all peanuts, butter beans and sugar! Everything, with the exception of the time you spend persuading, is overhead expense. You must prepare as much as you can but that prep-time doesn't generate cash. Cold calling kicks off the cash generation cycle that gets you the things that you want.

Being heard but not seen

The last part of this section concerns something you must take on board and work on very seriously as a cold call chicken. You see, just "saying some words off a script" is not what counts when cold calling or indeed with any form of verbal communication. When you are in front of another person you cannot help communicating with them. The process begins long before you open your mouth and actually speak the words that are forming in your mind. When you can see the other person and they can see you, over 55% of the other person's perception of you (and you of them) is derived from your mutual body language. The next most important factor is not in what you say but in the tone of your voice. In fact voice tone makes up another 35% of the other person's perception of you. So body language and voice tone combined, account for a staggering 90% of human communication leaving just 10% for the words themselves.

But during a telephone cold call, the person at the other end of the line cannot see you. On the other hand they can hear you. And it is the manner in which you speak the words combined with the tone of your voice that will influence the other person more than the actual content of your sales message. When on the telephone, 80% of the success or otherwise of your call is down to the tone of your voice.

In addition, listening to the way the person at the other end of the line responds to you will tell you more about what they are thinking and the way they process information than anything else. This particular skill will build as you become more experienced in cold calling but it is worth us spending a little time here examining these giveaway mannerisms and we will do that before the end of this section.

First how YOU say what you say

The main thing here is that you must work on keeping your voice "conversational." This may sound easy but if you're using notes or actually reading from a script it can be incredibly hard. In particular, if you have written the precise words you are going to say on a piece of paper, and you are not particularly experienced, you will probably find you have a tendency to steadily drop your voice toward the end of each sentence.

> The effect is that as you read each line your voice tone goes down and ends with an exclamation mark! Of course this is not the way we speak to each other when we are conversing but it is what usually happen when we read! It is particularly obvious when a call center cold caller contacts you at home and tries to get you to change your gas supplier! The impersonal feeling this communicates to us is a good chunk of the reason that most of us hate this type of cold call!

Another very common, speaking fault which implies uncertainty and lack of confidence, is a tendency to make statements or reply to questions in a manner of asking another question. For example, if a customer asks: "Yes this is Mr Head Honcho, what can I do for you?" It is common to hear a sales person reply: *"This is Jim Bloggs? Er ... of Western Widgets? ... We make the gizmos that are guaranteed to cut bearing wear by half?"*

The unnecessary, inbuilt, implied question is a turn-off for any listener. Nobody will ride into battle behind you if you, the trumpeter, sound an uncertain note. Your voice should inspire confidence even if you don't feel it. If you don't feel it then decide to act as if you do feel it. A few years ago I took flying lessons and my instructor gave me identical instructions for making radio transmissions. He told me always to sound confident on the radio whatever the circumstances. Even if I got lost he said, I should never broadcast the words, "I am lost" because that would make me, the speaker, and other pilots hearing my transmission, twice as nervous. Instead he told me to say: "I am temporarily unsure of my position" in the most confident voice I could muster and somebody out there would happily work with me. Having, indeed, been "temporarily unsure" on several occasions since, I have always found when you're "acting confident" it is accepted by others at face value despite what you're really feeling inside.

The manner of speaking which comes across as the most persuasive of all when the other person can't see you, is one which is conversational. The words you say should not be read word for word if it can be avoided. The best way to remind yourself what to say next, is to keep a sheet of bullet points by the phone to remind you. It is OK to write out a script during the planning stage and to practice using this with a friend or colleague. But when you pick up the phone to a real prospective customer try not to read all the words. In addition, you should place a big sign on the wall behind the telephone which says:

> **Stand up!**
> **Smile !**
> **Slow down !**
> **Speak deep !**

Stand up, because standing up, and even walking about while you are cold calling, will make you feel and sound more confident. **Smile**, because (surprisingly) you can hear a smile on the phone. **Slow down**, because 80% of cold callers speak too quickly to be heard clearly. **Speak deep**, because when combined with **Slow down**, a voice tone which is a tone deeper than most people's normal voice, is usually perceived as having both power and authority; the most persuasive combination of all. (*To make this easier just* *press one foot hard down on the floor while you speak. You will find that you both slow down and go deep!*)

How to analyze the other person from their voice

As you become more experienced at cold calling you will begin to notice that the people you are talking to process information in different ways and also react differently to you according to their character type. With information processing I have now realized that human beings have three different ways of doing this. We all make use of all three ways to some degree, yet one way dominates in each of our heads according to the way our brain works. In my experience the ways we process information are Visual, Aural or Textured.

Talking to a Visual

When a visual person speaks to me, he or she will use phrases such as: "Do you *see* what I mean?," "From the *look* of it...." So I reply, "Yes I get the picture." Because the prospective customer is processing information from the point of view of a visual personality, I reply using the same subconscious phraseology.

Talking to a Aural

The next person I cold call might say things like, "I know it sounds as if I'm whining" or, "Yes that rings a bell," and I realize that I'm talking to someone whose mental processing is built around "hearing" which makes them an "auditory" and I reply using the same type of language, "So you want to make a big bang then?"

Talking to a Textured

Then another client says, "This is a particularly rough patch for our business. We are up against a solid brick wall." So I reply, "So if we can smooth things out would you consider sliding our next course into your agenda?," because their processing system is built around a textured world.

I recently heard a poor exchange between a cold caller and a prospective customer in which each side used a different processing system which resulted in a total communications breakdown. In response to the customer saying, "No the outlook is rather dull at present" the seller replied, "I suppose you will just have to sit down with a cold towel round your head and work on the solution," to which the person at the other end reacted: "What? That would be really horrible and look pretty stupid wouldn't it!" The sales person was using a textured model when the prospect was clearly a visual. The call ended very quickly with no sale.

A bit of careful listening and an appropriately crafted response will get you a long way in cold calling. The simplest way to establish a subconscious link is to get inside your prospect's head and see the world from his or her perspective. By talking in the same way as your prospect and by using the same phraseology you automatically and subconsciously build trust. That trust is essential if you are trying to get the prospect to spend money with you. Put simply, we all tend to like people who are like us.

And there is one final thing you should know about the personalities you are likely to come across when you are cold calling. Broadly speaking there are four of them. I call them **Drivers**, **Expressives**, **Amiables**, and **Analytics**. Once you have gauged the type of personality you are talking to you can quite accurately predict the amount of time and effort you are going to have to spend getting a final decision.

Drivers

Tend to have a very physical and sometimes a bullying or an intimidating manner. They are found most often at the very top of large successful organizations usually as managing director or chief executive officer. Lately, the most obvious place to see them in the flesh has been on some of the sudden-death business reality-TV shows. The shows in which budding entrepreneurs perform tough tasks and either retain their place or get brutally eliminated by these seemingly humorless, tough guys. The great things about them are that they make very quick decisions and are not afraid to spend a lot of money!

Expressives

Expressives are more humane versions of drivers. They smile more and are less brutal but they are just as focused on succeeding and staying at the top. They can be very hard when it comes to making tough decisions but the victims are treated more benevolently. The great thing about expressives is that they also are not afraid to make quick decisions to spend money although they spend a little more time making the decision.

Amiables

Amiables tend to be found in the lower orders of staff inside any organization. They are easy to locate and talk to and as their "type" suggests, are very "amiable." The easiness and their approachability make them very popular with sales people and cold callers. Most seller's client records and contact sheets are made up of amiable names. There is only one problem … they have little power to make the spending decision you want. Sure they have power but it is only the power to say "no" rather than the power to say "yes." If you get in with an Amiable you are probably not going to get anywhere fast.

Analytics

Many middle-managers, accountants, engineers, technologists, and those who have more cerebrally based occupations, tend to be found in the category described as Analytic. They like mulling over the problems and issues that come their way. They enjoy the journey toward a solution rather than the final solution itself. They tend to dislike talking on the telephone for some reason and take a long time to make decisions. Once they have the initial information they need, they then look for the detail behind the information—then the detail behind the detail and so on. Even when they get sufficient, detailed information, they are rarely able to make the decision themselves and have to refer upward to a more senior person for final approval. Not too many great things about cold calling Analytics—it is going to be a hard slog.

From the table you can see that as a cold caller you should always aim for the **Drivers** and **Expressives** if you want a rapid decision. If you aim lower in an organization you will find yourself calling over and over again in order to get the same result you can often get from just 1 or 2 calls to the very top.

Personality summary table

Drivers	Expressives
Hard, bullying intimidating. Tend to occupy the very top positions in organizations. Sometimes, whether male or female, described as the 'M.A.N.' because they have a good prospect's essential attributes: **M**oney, **A**uthority, **N**eed.	Kindly, humorous, approachable. Tend also to occupy the upper echelons of management or are very successful entrepreneurs. Also have control over Money, have the Authority to spend it and have the Need for your product or service.
Not always pleasant to deal with but should be the cold callers' first target; they make buying decisions as a result of just 1 or 2 contacts from you.	Generally pleasant to deal with and should also be a first target for cold callers. They make buying decisions fast too but may take 2 to 3 contacts from you.
They make up just 15% of all contacts.	Also make up about 15% of all contacts.
Amiables	**Analytics**
Very friendly, easy, and approachable, although not, in general, particularly influential. Most sales people start a cold call at this level simply because it's "easy."	Not too keen on telephone conversations. Personalities vary between people with a chip on their shoulder and those who are reasonably approachable. Tend to prefer things and ideas more than people.
The big problem is that "Amiables" love to talk about everything under the sun but generally can't decide anything on their own except to say "no." Generally takes 3 to 5 calls to get any sort of a decision as a result of calling them.	Can rarely make final decisions and put off making decisions if they can. They often block decision making in case it's wrong. Generally takes 5 to 6 calls or more to get a decision.
Make up a whopping 35% of all contacts.	Make up another 35% of all contacts.

SECTION 3

We must believe in luck. For how else can we explain
the success of those we don't like?

JEAN COCTEAU – FRENCH DRAMATIST

Attitude

I'd like you to imagine for a moment that your boss (if you work for a company) or a fairy godmother philanthropist (if you work for yourself) has approached you with a proposition. They have told you that you can have a whole year off work, on full pay. Your position is guaranteed on your return provided you go off and do some good works for the next year. I am thinking of something like working overseas assisting with a disaster relief program, or installing fresh water supplies for remote communities in Africa, or working in your local town with the Salvation Army.

The one stipulation is that you must first write a job description for the person who will have to be recruited to replace you for the year that you're not there. So, I'd like you to write down, now, in the box below, as many of the qualities and skills you can think of, that would be necessary to make up the rounded personality who will be recruited to replace you. Don't turn the page until you've done this. Here are some descriptive words and phrases to start you off: product knowledge, sense of humor, good with numbers, sensitive, persistent, tenacious, not a clock watcher, selling skills, creative, positive attitude, a "do-er" not a procrastinator, written skills, language skills, problem solver, good telephone manner, desire to be the best, perseverance, a hero not a victim, market knowledge, likes other people etc. Keep going until you've included everything that it would take to make a clone of you.

Now I'd like you to look at all the words and phrases you've written in the box and mark next to each one an "**S**" for a **Skill** related word/phrase, an "**A**" for an **Attitude** related one and finally a "**K**" for anything that is **Knowledge** related.

What do you notice about your list? Do you see a very heavy bias, not toward "**K**nowledge" or "**S**kills" as you might expect, but instead, toward "**A**" for *Attitude*. This is not an accident or an outcome which varies widely between different people, cultures or groups.

Attitude

The longer I live, the more I realize the impact of attitude on life.

Attitude, is more important than facts. It is more important than the past, than education, than money, than circumstances, than failures, than successes, than what other people think or say or do. It is more important than appearance, giftedness or skill. It will make or break a company or a home. The remarkable thing is we have a choice everyday regarding the attitude we will embrace for that day. We cannot change our past ... we cannot change the fact that people will act in a certain way.

We cannot change the inevitable. The only thing we can do is play on the one string we have, and that is our attitude ... I am convinced that life is 10% what happens to me and 90% how I react to it. And so it is with you ... we are in charge of our attitudes.

CHARLES SWINDOLL

Want to succeed at life? Sort out your attitude first

The most important factor contributing toward the successes or failures of life, regardless of profession, sex, height, attractiveness, aptitude, skills, and knowledge, all boil down, eventually, to this one word: attitude. It applies as much to success in selling and in this case, cold calling, as to anything else.

As a long time sales professional I know this is true. I've seen more successful people in sales who were regularly rated "poor" when it came to product knowledge and "useless" when applying traditional selling skills. But their sales performances, year after year, were either on-target or way over target. I was also interested to see the same importance of this reflected in a TV documentary a couple of years ago.

"Are You Tough Enough?"

The program, broadcast over several weeks, was about regular members of the public who wanted to find out if they were good enough to join the SAS. The SAS (Special Air Service), as most people know, is the highly trained commando force of the British Army. They operate in small four-man units, behind enemy lines and often in extremely dangerous conditions. They have to be able to go for days through wet jungle undergrowth, feet covered in bleeding blisters ("Don't worry lads; it's only pain!"). Or cross open dry deserts, with only basic rations to sustain them, each carrying a load of equipment weighing almost as much as the soldier himself.

About 2000 members of the public joined the initial trials marching, walking, and running across the mountainous

Brecon Beacons in South Wales. Only about 20 men and women were left after this early stage and these few were flown out to the Malaysian jungle with an ex-SAS training officer—a short, tough, Scottish soldier. He was their trainer, mentor, and examiner; and at each stage, over several weeks, more and more people were eliminated from the competition by him and his support team of a military doctor and military psychologist.

Each task was genuinely more grueling than the previous one. No punches were pulled. As they progressed through the jungle the tasks involved some hair-raising exercises and immense fatigue. There was hand-to-hand fighting or "milling" to build aggression, sleep deprivation, swimming and marching with full kit, and a scarily realistic interrogation after being captured by the "enemy." In the end there were just four people left: three men and one woman. These were paraded in front of a real SAS team of four experienced serving soldiers. All four SAS soldiers had their faces fogged out to avoid identification; they were the genuine article. They were then asked to perform a single task: "You have observed all these people in action over the past few weeks. We now need you to select one as the outright winner of this whole project. That person should be the one who you would have as part of a four-man SAS patrol."

Without hesitation they unanimously chose the woman. She hadn't been the strongest throughout, neither was she the best educated. She had not even performed best in all the exercises. However, she had the one thing they identified as the most important of all when the chips were down in real life-threatening situations.

"She had," they said, "*the right attitude.*"

"This is the life we have chosen" (Don Corelone *The Godfather*)

So what's this really got to do with selling and cold calling? When we are involved with selling things to other people we are rarely, if ever, placed in life-threatening situations. Nevertheless we have to put up with endless "no's," turn downs, rejections, unexpected cancellations, and regular rudeness on the road to whatever it is we want from the job (more about this later). Sellers of all descriptions get big rewards, commissions, and bonuses not for the deals they close but in return for all the rejection they will inevitably receive on the way. This is where our individual need for ways to access the right attitude comes in.

Large sales-orientated organizations have done, and still do regular surveys and research to find out what they need to look for in candidates for jobs that involve selling. Time and again the pie chart for the make up of successful sales people looks like this:

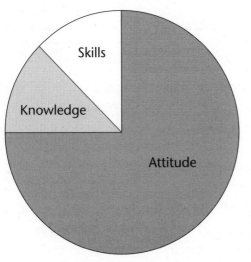

What counts most in the success pie?

So what are you going to do about yours?

Well, first, I am assuming that you still want to be a success at selling and specifically at the cold calling part. You do? Well in that case the news is good—you can be.

Even if you have never sold anything before, simply knowing that you want to succeed is enough to begin with. A lot of people, including some of my adult friends are not sure what they want out of life. I asked one of them recently (he's in his fifties like me, but not in sales) if he wanted to be a success. He said, "It's too late now." I then asked him if he had ever wanted to be a success. He said, "Not really ... just happy." I then asked him if, in his middle age, he thought life had been disappointing. He replied, "I suppose it has really."

Now it may be a shock to you but not everyone has a desire to succeed like you. Some people are content—or think they are—just to get by. The reality is that in their teens they expected it all to just "happen" and end up finding they've been waiting for a bus that never arrived.

An idiot walked into the bank
And asked with the greatest of ease,
"I'd like to take out a thousand pounds in
twenty pound notes, if you please."
The bank clerk replied, "Ah, well, well, well!
You must pardon me Sir if I grin.
But you cannot take anything out of the bank.
For you have not put anything in."

(ANON)

It's rather like the exchange between Felix and Oscar in the movie *The Odd Couple*. Oscar, arrives home late for dinner and asks Felix to get some gravy to make the meat moist. Felix asks, "Where am I going to get gravy at 8 o'clock?" Oscar replies, "I don't know. I thought it comes when you cook the meat." Which causes the exasperated Felix to explode, "*When you cook the meat?* ... You don't know what you're talking about. You just don't know, because you've got to make gravy. It doesn't come!"

> **"The mass of men live lives of quiet desperation"**
> HENRY THOREAU

The reality is that most people are just too lazy and fearful to make the things they want to happen "happen." But, speaking as a fundamentally lazy man (not to mention a cold calling chicken) myself, I have to tell you that getting a powerful selling attitude sorted out, actually doesn't require too much effort or courage. I'm going to tell you now how I learned to do it and set out all you need to do if you want the same.

Attitude rule 1: The important thing about a goal is having one

After my first three months at Xerox, Bruce carried out my initial appraisal. Half way through he stopped and said, "Tell me why you decided to take this job?" I replied, "So that I can make some money, have a nice house, a decent car ... you know." "That's your next problem," he said, "you're like a lot of people in the world. They've taken the first step toward the life they want by just making up their mind to do something different. Then they take the second step by deciding to stay away from everybody (the majority) who can tell them every reason they won't succeed. But it's still all too vague for real mind-blowing success. You now need to really kick-start your winning attitude. The best way I can show you how to do that is to get you to join me in a little improvised role-play. Pretend for a moment that you're the agent on an airline ticket desk, and I'll be the erstwhile passenger, OK?" I agreed and this is what happened:

Passenger (Bruce): I'd like to buy a ticket please.

Agent (Me): *Certainly Sir....where to?*

Passenger: You know.

Agent: *I'm sorry Sir could you be a little more explicit?*

Passenger: Yes certainly ... somewhere nice ... where I'll be very happy.

Agent: *And where's that exactly Sir?*

Passenger: You KNOW!! ... where the sun is shining ... and I'll have a great day ... look would you hurry please I haven't got much time!!

Agent: *I'm really sorry Sir but...*

Passenger: Look. I want to end up somewhere nice. I want to be where there are people I like and in a culture I fit in with ... Oh, and I want the type of accommodation I like. ... Please give me that ticket or I'll miss the flight!

So here's the big question posed by Bruce's little role play. Why can't the ticket agent sell the passenger a ticket?

The answer is blindingly obvious of course. The agent can't sell the passenger a ticket because he doesn't know where he's trying to go. But that is the problem with most people's lives—they're not getting anywhere because they have no clear idea where they want to get to.

Just like the passenger who wants to get to "somewhere nice," wanting to have *nice* car, a *great* house, *lots* of money or a *good-looking* partner, is probably a recipe for arriving somewhere you didn't actually want to go.

I hope you're doing this thing called "selling" to bring you the life you want. This is because life is just waiting for you to tell it exactly what it is you want, in detail. Otherwise the best you can hope for is a mystery tour.

Now, at the time Bruce told me that I had to get a clear, explicit goal in my head, in order to develop the right "attitude" for selling, I had just got my first mortgage. (They were very keen on big mortgages among the salesforce because it meant one *had* to work hard in order to pay it.) So, the goal I fixed on was to be able to pay it by achieving my minimum, company-imposed, sales target on a monthly basis, and to never have to play "catch-up" because I had slipped behind in any month. Well, I set and achieved the goal. The activity of "goal setting" had proved itself to me. It worked well—it was clear and measurable. I got what I wanted. But I didn't realize how close I was to achieving a lot more in life. In fact, I was very close to a method, almost a formula, for getting everything in life I had ever wanted by just expanding that basic idea. That discovery took me another nine years. This is what happened.

The lazy person's route to wealth

After several years at Xerox I decided to embark upon a new career as a trader in the London financial market. It was quite an experience and I loved it but it's not particularly relevant to this book. After another five years in this field I was approached by a growing company supplying electronic information services to the financial market: Reuters. They made me an offer to take up a position as a sales executive selling their products. It was the late 1970s and right at the leading edge of the electronic information revolution. It was an exciting opportunity but having not been in front-line sales for five years I thought I should try to get "re-motivated." To do this I asked an old friend and very successful salesman exactly what method he followed in order to become so consistently successful. He looked at me for a long time and then told me he would show me what he did if I promised (faithfully) not to laugh. I agreed and this is what he shared with me.

Everything you ever wanted

He called his method "The lazy person's route to wealth." He told me anyone could do it. It wasn't at all difficult. It was extremely simple and uncannily effective. Yet most people thought it was daft, so even when they heard about it they failed to do anything. I am now a huge fan of this method and have outlined the main points for you below. It is up to you to consider whether and how to apply them in your own life. Everybody I have introduced these methods to, and who has then gone on to apply them consistently, has had the same results as me—truly amazing! The core of his method I was already familiar with, and was one I had learned from Bruce Cantle at Xerox: the importance of having a clear goal or goals in life. However, this method took the whole concept to a new—and for me life-changing—level.

Write it down...

First, it was more than about having a single goal. The first idea in the "lazy person" method is that it is very important to get all the goals you have for your life down on paper. (By the way, it makes no difference whether you believe in the method or not. I can testify that it has worked for everybody I know who has actually done it.) There is apparently something very powerful psychologically about writing down what it is you want in life. My friend told me that it is supposed to be based on some research carried out at an American university back in the 1950s, in which half a class were asked to write down their aspirations for the 10 years after they left the college. The other half was asked to do nothing at all. The first group were contacted again when the 10 years had passed and the researchers found that over three-quarters of them had achieved their goals and in many cases much more. Out of the other half of the class, those who had not written down their goals, less than a quarter had achieved them.

So back to you. Your first step on the road to moving toward everything you want in your life, supported by the all-important right attitude, is to spend some time, right now, thinking about exactly what it *is* that you want. Once you've worked this out write down each goal on a sheet of paper. This is very important—don't sit there and "think" it will just happen—you must write it down.

Not just materialistic ...

Take some time out now to think about and write down all the materialistic and spiritual things you want out of your life. There should be no limitations on this—if somebody ... another human being ... is able to have the things you want, you can have them too, believe me. So at this stage don't place any limitation on the life you want, just write it all down, one item at a time.

But don't be daft ...

Now just one word of caution ... don't be stupid about goal setting. It's no good thinking you can break the laws of physics with this exercise. Therefore don't set a goal, for example, that you will be able to stand on top of the nearest high building, flap your arms, and jump off and you'll be able to fly. If you do that you ARE going to die! In a similar vein, it's no good setting a goal that you'll become a member of the Royal family, because it is not possible for you or me! Or that, as a 40-year-old person (if you are one), you will be able to run a 4-minute mile! Just make sure that your goal is physically possible but at the same time challenging. Most people

I know set smallish goals: a slightly bigger house with an extra bedroom … a second-hand Porsche … an extra 30% added to their bank balance. This is just not good enough my dear cold call chicken—you need some really big goals.

Don't worry about how these really big goals will manifest themselves in your life. They will … leave that bit to me. Just write them down (as I did, full of scepticism a few years ago. At the end of this section I am going to share some of my first goals with you and tell you exactly what happened). Just make them goals that a human can achieve … then wait and see.

Just add in the detail …

Once you've made your list, sit back and consider each one of your goals and add in a lot of detail. For example, if one of your goals is a house, then write down exactly how big it is. What style is it, modern or period? How big is the garden? What color is the front door? You need all the detail you can think of.

If another goal is a new car, set down not only the make but the color as well and all the other things you want like leather seats, convertible, GPS and so on. If it's money exactly how much do you want? "A lot" isn't good enough … you need to decide an exact amount. A goal doesn't have to be something materialistic either. Let's say you want to retire in 10 years to enable you to spend your life managing a charity, or living in a religious commune somewhere, write down exactly what you see yourself doing in this role, where you'll be, and what you'll be doing.

Write as if it's already happened and set a date for completion

The next thing you need to do, is go through each goal and rewrite it as if it has already happened and set a date for its completion. So instead of writing down "I want a Bentley Continental painted silver with cream leather seats and maroon piping, GPS navigation, rear seat entertainment system and 20-inch chrome alloy wheels" instead write, "It is January 1st 20xx and I have just taken delivery of my new Bentley Continental. It is silver in color, with cream leather seats, edged with maroon piping and has a full GPS system with a full rear seat entertainment system ..." and so on. Write each goal in precisely the same way, in detail, with a date for completion for each one.

Repeat at least once a day

You've done all that? ... good—but just writing your goal list is not the end of it. The next bit is very simple but it requires daily application. Each day, when you get up in the morning, take your goal list out of your wallet or purse, go through each goal and read it out to yourself.

Don't just read it in your head ... you need to move your lips and, if you can, actually say the words out loud. Once you've done that and before you move on to the next goal, close your eyes and get a picture in your mind of the goal. See it. Feel it. Feel the emotion. Really get involved in your mind's eye.

This is all based on a very sound psychological principle that your subconscious mind does not know the difference between reality and imagination. If you don't believe me try this very simple test. ... Imagine that you are holding in the fingertips of one hand half a fresh lemon. Hold this imaginary lemon so that it is face-up. Now give it a squeeze and watch as the imaginary juice oozes down the side of the lemon skin. Feel the cold sticky juice run down your fingers. Give it an extra squeeze and see the little curtain of juice mist over the lemon and smell it in the air. Give it another good squeeze and as you do so bring the hand holding the lemon toward your lips and stick out your tongue. As your fingers bring the lemon close to your tongue what is happening in your mouth? … Don't tell me … there is more saliva in there and your mouth is really watering just as if there is a real lemon there. As Einstein said, "When imagination and reality are in conflict your imagination always wins. Imagination is much more important than reality."

Doing this goal reading, repeating and imagining each day (once in the morning and again in the evening if you can), establishes a pattern in your mind. Just as leading sports people and athletes now use sports psychology based on similar imagination techniques, you are tapping in to exactly the same strange power. Your brain starts to believe, whether you like it or not, that you are already able to manifest these things in your life. This seems to set up a sort of unconscious radar in your head, so that when you are going about your normal daily business, your brain is constantly, subconsciously searching and working on turning your goals into reality.

And finally something not to do

If you decide that you want to use the same "lazy person" method for yourself, there is one final word of caution I would like to place before you. It is this: do not tell anybody you are doing this if you think they will laugh! Laughter and derision are the biggest enemies of successful new ventures. As a bit of a self-confessed chicken you will probably be susceptible to ribbing and jokes about something that appears, on the surface, to be just a bit too easy to have any chance of success. Yet goal setting and persistent visualization in the way that I have just described are really powerful and extremely effective. The only people who will laugh are those whose lives are not as successful as they would like (the "hopium" addicts). The really successful people in life will not laugh at all

Let me repeat ...

This goal setting activity is very important in order to start getting your attitude sorted out. It isn't difficult, in fact, it's quite a simple procedure—but don't let this simplicity fool you. Above all, do not tell anybody who might laugh at the simplicity of the method, that you are doing this. Their laughter may well put you off. It works ... never mind the cynics. In fact, the only people who will tell you that it won't be effective are the people who are not particularly successful themselves.

If you're still doubtful ... what happened with my 1979 goal list?

I said earlier that I would share what happened as a result of my writing my very first goal list back in 1979. When I wrote that first list I set down 17 goals in total.

I went through all the procedures outlined for you previously, and I did this everyday. Time passed and life happened. In fact, nearly 20 years passed before I saw the original list again.

I was in the Hertz car rental office at San Francisco Airport. The year was 1997. I was running a training unit for Reuters in America and had agreed to fly across from the east coast to give some coaching in presentation skills. This meant that when I arrived at the airport I was laden down with cameras, tripods, microphones and all the other paraphernalia of the job—so I decided to rent a car to carry it all.

While I was standing at the rental desk filling in the forms the desk clerk looked them all over then said, "May I see your drivers license please?" I reached in my jacket pocket, pulled out my ancient leather wallet and searched inside for the license. When I located it, I pulled it out and handed it to her. As I did so, a dog-eared piece of paper came with it and fell on the floor—it was that original list. I stood there nostalgically reading through it and I was stunned!

By the way: something weird happened to me while I was writing this book

Because I use these methods myself I had written down, as a recent goal, that I would open up part of my business in a particular Middle-Eastern city. I had never worked in the city or spoken to anybody about this plan before. Within 24 hours of writing it down I received, out of the blue, a call from a potential client in that city requesting a proposal for a training program. Three days later I received an unconnected request from a university in the same city to make a paid address to an E-business marketing conference at the same time. That same night traveling to London Heathrow airport in a cab en-route to another assignment, I was talking to a colleague about these events on my cellphone. When I finished my call the cab driver spoke to me: "I couldn't help overhearing you call," he said, "I'm from that city and my cousin is a senior diplomat in my country. I know he would be willing to give you some inside information on our culture and customs, and make any introductions you require so that you can expand your business. We are very hungry for the sort of skills you offer." The point is, this sort of coincidence doesn't happen just sometimes. When you start to practice this method you will find that exactly things start happening in your life. Don't ask why. Just do it!

As I read through it I realized that during the 10 years following my writing of the list, I had achieved every single one of my original goals. As an example I'll share just one of them with you.

As God is my witness, back in 1979, I wrote the following goal as if it had already been achieved: *"It is April 1987 and I have just purchased for £250,000 a large, detached, five-bedroom house just outside London. It has a large garage, a spacious tree-lined garden with a miniature steam railway running round the perimeter."*

Back then, I couldn't imagine how that, or any of the other goals (including learning to fly, buying an apartment near Bond Street in London, and setting up the business I have now) were going to manifest themselves in my life, but the deal was that I should write them down with no limitation, so I did.

Today, I live in precisely the house I described, visualized and repeated to myself all those years ago … and the steam locomotive is terrific! This goal setting stuff just seems to work. The coincidences that start emerging when you tell life clearly, and in detail, what you want are extraordinary. As somebody very wise once said, "Be careful what you pray for because you could well find yourself getting it!"

I should add one more bit of proof for you which followed on directly after my San Francisco revelation. Standing there in the car rental office I decided to test the long forgotten method once again. I took from my pocket my airline ticket stub from the flight I'd just taken from the east coast and wrote across the back of it: "It is September 1st 1997 (*three months later*) and $5000 has come into my bank account from an unexpected source." Each day, for the next few weeks, I would, at least once a day, get the stub from my wallet, read that goal silently to myself, then visualize the money. In my mind's eye I would imagine my bank statement with the deposit in it for a few seconds then get on with my day. What happened next was remarkable once again.

About five weeks after writing the new goal I had to fly from New York to Chicago on business. As I took my seat on the plane the passenger seated next to me said, "Good morning." When I replied he heard from my accent that I wasn't an American. He actually asked, as so often happens when Americans hear a British accent, if I was Australian. Having got me talking, he went on to ask my name and what I did for a living. When I told him that I was in charge of teaching sales techniques to a large multinational he became very interested. "We need to get better at selling in my business," he said, "I'm senior partner in a Chicago law firm ... how would you feel about running a sales training workshop for us?" I told him I was a full-time employee and couldn't really give up the time. "What about over a weekend?" he said, "We'll fly you out to Chicago on a Friday night and back on a Sunday evening! All expenses paid on top of that. So what would your training fee be?" "Five thousand dollars," I replied. "Done!" he said shaking my hand. Three weeks later I ran the weekend workshop!

Now where did all that come from? Why was I seated next to that particular man on that particular flight? What made me say $5000? I can't tell you what is behind this particular goal setting technique. And I'm certainly not saying that it happens every single time and for every single goal that I have set. It is just that the vast majority of the time (in my experience about 80% of the time—remember the Pareto principle!), the goals I set really *do* manifest themselves in remarkable ways. I still do it regularly. You should too ... just don't tell anybody!

Too weird for this book? I'll chance it

The British TV game show host Noel Edmonds did not have a TV show for nearly 10 years and had been through a number of difficult personal situations. Then in 2005 he began using basically the same method, I have outlined in this section. In media interviews in the Spring of 2006 he called it "Cosmic Ordering."

He said that during 2005 he had written down six things he wanted. Among them were to get back into TV and find a house with very specific qualities in France. Within months he says, he was, out of the blue, offered a brand new TV show, "Deal or No Deal" (which has since been nominated a number of awards), had found the house in France he'd been dreaming of and achieved two other "private" desires.

Personally I don't care what he calls it. I judge on results alone and it looks to me as if the basic idea is identical to mine. So what have you got to lose? If it works don't mend it.

Attitude rule 2: Never underestimate the power of persistence

The next step, my dear cold call chicken, is to let you in on another dirty little secret: most of your competitors just like most of mine, give up much too soon. They do a minimal amount of cold calling, if they do any at all, then they stop as soon as they can. Yet successful people the world over identify "persistence" as one enduring differentiator of successful people.

The British wartime Prime Minister Sir Winston Churchill ferociously underscored the requirement that, in order to succeed, one must "Never, never, never, give up." Thomas

Edison, inventor of the electric light bulb had to carry out over one thousand experiments before he succeeded in his quest. Somebody once asked him if he ever became discouraged by his constant failures. He replied that he never had done because from his point of view he had simply learned a thousand ways *not* to make a light bulb.

Ray Kroc the man who founded McDonalds is reputed to have had a large sign hanging on his office wall underlining the importance of persistence. He in turn apparently copied it from Calvin Coolidge, US President in the 1930s who said:

Persistence

Nothing in the world can take the place of persistence. Talent will not; nothing is more common than unsuccessful men with talent. Genius will not; unrewarded genius is almost a proverb. Education will not; the world is full of educated derelicts. Persistence and determination alone are omnipotent. The slogan "Press on" has solved and always will solve the problems of the human race.

I read recently about some experiments done in a British university in the past few years which involved some very successful business people being given a large-scale puzzle made of lightweight interconnecting plastic blocks (a large-scale version of the small wooden cube puzzles available in novelty stores). The puzzle was almost impossible to solve in large scale. A group of averagely successful people in the same room were given the same puzzle to solve at the same time. After about 12 minutes or so the average people had given up trying to solve it. However, in the case of the successful business people they were still working on it 45 minutes later. In fact, the researchers almost had to tear the puzzle from their hands so tenacious were they in their quest to solve it.

When I began selling I always remembered the poster below which used to hang on our sales office wall. It combined two important ideas related to persistence and fear of cold calling and for this reason it also hangs on my office wall today:

The Canticle for Cold Calling

Where am I now?
Sitting in front of the phone

What do I want to do?
Call a prospect to sell him my product

What is the worst thing he can say?
"No"

What is the worst thing he can do?
Put the phone down

Then where will I be?
Sitting in front of the phone

So what am I waiting for?

On average it takes six "cold calls" before any one prospect will do business with you:

95% of all sales people make the first cold call
50% of all sales people make the second cold call
25% of all sales people make the third cold call
15% of all sales people make the fourth cold call
10% of all sales people make the fifth cold call

and

just **5%** of all sales people make the **sixth** cold call
and they take **85%** of the available new business in
any market.

To keep me persisting (I'm just as inclined to give up as you if I'm not careful) I have managed to find a nice little motivator for me based on some very recent research into the way our human brains recall things. It seems that much of what we remember is held in pictures in our heads. If somebody mentions a familiar word or phrase we tend to instantly form a picture of it. For instance, if somebody says "World Trade Center" most adults immediately see a mental image of the scene they witnessed on 9/11. The image is very often recalled as if it was on a TV screen—exactly as many people saw it, rather than up close as if it were right next door. They see the fire and all the other things that remind them of that awful day.

The persistence-generating fruit machine

In the same way the words "fruit machine" conjure up an image, in my mind, of a brightly lit "one-armed bandit" with spinning reels and a chance to win some money ... maybe even the jackpot. Like most people I don't mind having a go if I have a few extra coins in my pocket. I may win and then again I may not. Only one thing is certain: if I don't put some coins in and have a go then I'm definitely not going to win anything. It's just the same in my mind with cold calling. If I don't pick up the phone and dial the number (put the coins in the slot) then I'm not going to have a single chance of talking to a possible new prospective customer (the jackpot).

So, on the Internet I found a full color picture of a one-armed bandit and printed it out on a piece of card. Now whenever I feel jaded or bored or get tired or start slipping into a nonpersistent frame of mind (I'm a cold call chicken after all) I stand my one-armed bandit picture up in front of the telephone. Doing this I instantly get the full image and feelings I associate with the machine rather than the mundane telephone. I find it serves as an instant boost and gets me back on track by turning the boring phone into a real business generator. It may sound cheesy I know, but what the hell … it works!!

One last point. Although I enjoy an occasional gambling punt and therefore have no trouble with gambling pictures, I guess that some readers won't feel the same way. So if that includes you, you can easily substitute a gambling picture with one that suits you better. I have a client in America who has a picture of a baseball pitcher's mound and another in the UK who has a picture of a set of cricket stumps. In both cases the idea is the same; the pictures generate in the minds of those two a situation in which it is not necessary to hit the ball every time in order to win the game. But then again, if you don't take regular swipes at it then there is no chance at all staying in the game. Nobody but you can stand at the crease and take the shots. So get your picture organized as soon as you can!

> The Great Buddah was greeting a new arrival to one of the realms of Heaven and showing him round. At one point they passed a great room filled with gifts. "What are all those gifts Great Buddah?" asked the new arrival. "They are all the things that people prayed for in their lives" replied the Great Buddah, "But gave up just before they were about to be granted them."

Attitude rule 3: Stand tall and smile

I saw a cartoon once in which a little dog (I think it was Snoopy) was walking along with a big grin on his face. The little boy (Charlie Brown) asked him how he was feeling. The dog said that he had had a tough day and had earned the right to feel depressed. Charlie Brown queried the grin on his face and Snoopy replied that he really wanted to be depressed but he was finding it very difficult as he kept putting the "smiling face" on.

I challenge you right now to stand up and look at the sky (if you're on public transport best wait until you get home) and put a big cheesy grin on your face. Force it if you have to and keep it there however stupid you feel ... now, while you do this, try to think a really depressing thought.

Tough isn't it? It is very difficult to feel down even if you're just "acting happy." So, whatever else happens, a quick remedy for any low feeling is to get moving, smile and pretend just for a few minutes that you're not. Very soon, miracle of miracles, you'll probably find that you're not!

A survey printed in one of the London newspapers recently revealed that one thing optimistic people do constantly is to "look up" and move their bodies more enthusiastically than their pessimistic cousins. Hardly ground breaking stuff is it? But I find that, particularly when I'm cold calling, I push my chair into the corner and stride about the room. In fact I do most of my cold calling from my kitchen! Why? A.) because it's not the office—where there are no customers and too many distractions, and B.) although it's a kitchen (and you know what I think about "work" kitchens) there are no chairs to sit on so I have to stay on my feet to do it. No depression—more energy—better attitude.

What else affects the attitude of ambitious chickens?

Do you really want to?

Some business people want all the benefits of a selling career (including cold calling) but *none* of the emotional effort, risk and front-line work that goes with it. They are not at ease in any selling situation. In fact, they feel downright uneasy doing this thing that every commercial enterprise *has* to do. As far as I know this could be you. Many people hate sales people—even some authors who write and research the profession (not me). Some parents hate the thought of their offspring being in sales. If you fit in to any of these categories you have to find a way to address the issue.

Are you secretly scared of how great you could become?

Many chickens I know are quite capable of becoming truly great sales people but they stay in their comfort zone of "average performance" because they feel undeserving of the things a big breakthrough would bring them. If this is you see a confidence counselor, a hypnotist, a therapist. Don't just sit there. Help is available!

"Here be dragons!"

The Vikings used to write this on the edge of their maps when they couldn't see or imagine what was over the horizon. They imagined all manner of fiends and devils would be waiting for them just the other side.

Listen, I've been shouted at. I've had people put the phone down on me. They still do. Just about every sales person I ever met in 35 years has had the same experience at one time or another. The reason sales people are paid well is precisely because of all the "no's" they have to take. Nobody is waiting by the phone for your cold call and you may, therefore, just catch a few people just at the wrong moment. No's are an inevitable part of the job. As Don Corelone said in *The Godfather* "This is the life we have chosen!"

You will have people say all sorts of rotten things to you when you cold call, you just need to make sure you don't say them to yourself. Self-talk is very important. Get a picture of a smiling prospect in your head. Expect the person at the other end of the line to be happy. Get a happy feeling inside you. Lucky people expect to be lucky. By deciding to have a good feeling inside you, you'll find you can handle whatever is thrown at you.

They probably won't want my stuff

Products and services which "sell" are solutions to somebody's problem. Identify the problems your product is designed to fix. Make sure you cold call the type of potential customer who might have the sort of problem you can solve.

You're paralyzed

Many sales people are just like you. They deeply desire to make it happen but their imagination paints a picture of all the inevitable problems on the way. It's push–pull inside their head all the time. They are attracted to the life that a lot of cold calling will give them but are held back by thoughts of failure. I've seen sales people sit in offices with a phone to their ear listening to the dial tone "pretending" to make calls. Their cold calling days are peppered with displacement activities. These paralyzed sales people get into work promising themselves to really get on with it ... Today! Really! ... but first they'll just get a coffee ... well not just a company coffee ... a shop downstairs coffee ... probably a Starbucks. Yes a Starbucks that will get rid of the nerves! The local Starbucks is quite a walk but the walk itself will also help with the nerves ... yes, then they'll definitely feel better ... definitely!

When they eventually get back to the desk they make a start ... they prepare the cold calling list for today ... well you DO have to get organized ... that takes time to do properly. By the time the "organization" bit is done of course it's getting on for lunchtime and nobody wants calls just before lunch so it'll have to wait until after lunch ... then ... then "I'll really start!" and so on and so on.

Each of these displacement activities is supposed to somehow "deal with the butterflies." The poor paralyzed chicken is hoping that a miracle will happen. That somehow the longer picking-up-the-phone is put off, the fewer butterflies will be left. My experience is that this strategy doesn't work. So what does un-paralyze a cold call chicken? The solution is so simple.

Here's the chicken's way to get over it

If the above is anything like the things you do in an attempt to get rid of the lily-livered, chicken-ness you often feel, you've reached the heart of what this book is all about. In fact it's why we called it *Cold Calling for Chickens*. Because I'm about to show you how to stay a Chicken, become a worse

Chicken and come out the other side less scared than you've ever been.

Paradoxical intention

At the end of WWII a Jewish psychologist, named Viktor E. Frankl, emerged from a Nazi concentration camp. His whole family had perished and he wrote a book entitled *Man's Search for Meaning* about the ways he found to handle the terror and trauma of the experience. The book is still in print and you will probably find it as inspiring and uplifting as I did. The part of it that you and I can make immediate use of is contained in the second half of the book entitled "Logotherapy in a nutshell." Reading this section you will come upon a theory that Frankl calls, "The law of paradoxical intention."

In broad terms, the law of paradoxical intention sets out an effective approach for dealing with any situation which is causing feelings of great fearfulness and trepidation. The essence of the law is that you should *not* try to eliminate fearful feelings by acting brave, or try to get rid of the butterflies with endless cups of coffee or other displacement activities.

Instead you should do everything in your power to try and make yourself feel worse! The best way to do this is through a little "method acting." How do you do this? It is simple but just a bit crazy!

Find yourself somewhere quiet. A room with a lockable door in which you can not be observed and in which you can be pretty sure nobody will disturb you for 10 minutes or so. Then, in this completely secure environment, physically act out the part of a real coward! Nobody can see or hear you so go-ahead, do whatever you would do if you were a seriously scared, trembling cold call chicken!! Hyperventilate ... cry ... sob ... roll on the floor ... rock backward and forward ... curl up in a corner in a fetal position ... pull at your hair. ... knot your hanky over and over ... it is completely up to you. It is your terror fantasy. Hold nothing back ... why should you? Nobody else can see you. Do this, without pause for between 5 and 10 minutes ... then stop.

You will discover something marvelous has happened. You will not feel frightened any more! Think of whatever was making you feel fearful before (cold calling in your case) and you'll discover that the feeling of terror has completely dissipated. You will need to repeat this at regular intervals just to remind your psyche that "chicken" is indeed what you need to stay. In fact, I want you to go one stage further, just like I do, and get yourself a plain, white index card. It should measure about 4 in × 6 in (10 cm by 15 cm). Now write across the front in large letters the following:

Place the card in front of your telephone whenever you are about to cold call. Psychologists call this well known phenomenon The Law of Paradoxical Intention. Now I cannot explain to you how any of this works. Or why the physical acting-out of an anticipated bad situation makes most of the fear just vanish. I can, however, tell you about a terrific example that came about after one of our Cold Calling for

Chickens seminars in London three years ago. At the end of many of these sessions a few people hang about to ask some final questions or clarify various points. On this occasion, I was approached by a large man, very rough looking, who told me he was opening an emergency plumbing business in north London. He had come to the seminar to pick up a few tips on getting the message out about his new business. "I know about all this stuff," he said, "actually I think a lot of it's a load of crap … I just wanted to tell you. (*gee thanks!*) but there's only one problem," he said. "I know I DO have to do some cold calling and I HATE it. So here's the deal! I'm going to give your paradoxical *"method"* a whirl for the next few weeks. If it don't work you can give me my money back. Deal?"

Well, as "Money back if not delighted" is part of our customer service strategy I had no trouble agreeing to this, even if I didn't fancy being worked over by him and some of his buddies if I failed in this regard. Two weeks later my phone rang … it was him again. "Mr Evrington? Yeah? I came to your seminar do you remember me?" (*How could I forget?*) Well I just thought I should let you know … your paradoxical chicken thing … it works! HOW?"

I have to say, I was unable to tell him. In the same way that I don't know how gravity works, or how electricity comes out of a socket in the wall, or why buttered toast always falls on the floor face down … it just does. So give it a go yourself and see what I mean. After all what have you got to lose? … You big cold call chicken!

SECTION 4

There is nothing more important to any business than sales. Without a sale nothing else matters.

BILLY HOLMES – SALES TRAINING MANAGER,
RANK XEROX UK 1970

Telling isn't selling

"Socrates was a man who went around giving people
advice—so they killed him."
11-YEAR-OLD CHILD'S ANSWER WHEN ASKED
TO DESCRIBE THE PHILOSOPHER

Many people whose job involves "selling" have been on
courses, have read books or listened to tapes and CDs, or
have scoured Internet sites in order to get a few tips on the
subject. The problem is that a lot of what is currently available is based on old-school methods (see page 13) and won't
be particularly effective if applied in the 21st century.
Alternatively, if the information is up-to-date and designed
for use in a modern market, it is read, viewed or listened to
(according to the available media) then largely ignored. The
receivers of the information sincerely believe that they know
better and have no need to follow the recommendations in
any of the books. They believe that their product or service is
different and that there is little need for them to become
familiar with up-to-date, validated, and proven methods of
selling.

When most humans try to persuade other humans to do something they tend to "have a go" at doing it by telling, talking-at, pitching, and presenting. They yap and yap and yap little realizing how rapidly the human mind on the receiving end of their pitch tunes out.

The plain fact is that the average human brain is fickle and easily bored. However good an individual sales person believes they are at making the greatest all-time successful "pitch," if the other brain isn't constantly stimulated and directly involved in the interchange there will be little or no effective communication. To put it another way, and in the context of this book which is specifically about cold calling, your prospect on the other end of the telephone line will "tune out" not in two minutes

"... not one and a half minutes ... not even one minute!

Your prospect's mind will start to wander in less than 30 seconds if you make a classic 'pitch' phone call. "

This is why over 90% of decision makers will tell you that they endeavor never to answer a cold call, and almost as many cannot remember ever having received a cold call that offered anything appropriate to their business at that time. The reason that we have this problem can best be visualized by looking at the diagram below which represents the prospective customer's point of view before receiving a call from a seller. Perhaps there is small problem somewhere which is possibly one of many. Maybe the cold caller has a solution to it. However, to date, it has not proved important enough for the buyer to spend much time effort or money to fix.

Once an average cold caller manages to get through to the potential buyer the tendency is to rapidly pitch, yap, talk, and generally talk, talk, talk, some more about the product or service they want the potential customer to buy. The

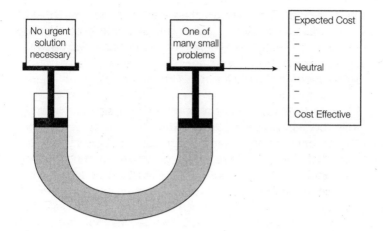

things that get talked about are the features of the service—what it is, how it works, how long they've been in business, how many customers they have, how big or small it is, the efficiency, the speed, the reliability. The pitch usually goes something like this

"Oh good morning, is that Mr Prospect? Yes? How are you today Sir? Great!! Mr Prospect, my name is Jose Indecipherable. This is just a courtesy call. I'm with Grinders Storage. Have you heard of us? No!? Well we're a local self-storage company, not the largest by any means, but we try harder (ha ha). As a storage company we are able to offer you many different sized units from 10 cubic meters to 1000 cubic meters at very competitive rates. All our units are security protected and guarded 24/7. Every unit is clean, dry and every customer is provided with their own padlock and key ... but you are at liberty to provide your own if you wish. We provide access Monday to Friday from 6am to 8:30pm and weekends from 7am to 7pm. Out of hours access is by special arrangement and there may be a fee payable but it is only nominal so nothing to worry about. And I should also tell you that use of our

internal transport facilities—forklift trucks etcetera—is included in the price and we can also quote you for external transport from your premises to ours and vice versa … if you need it. We have been established in this part of the country for over 10 years We already have a lot of local businesses on our books which are already regular customers of ours and we were wondering whether or not you would have any use for us at any time? … possibly … soon … or maybe sometime in the future? Mr Prospect? Are you still there? How much does all this cost? Well it varies according to what you want. Perhaps I could make an appointment maybe? … No? … Send you a brochure? Of course I will … but you don't have any need for us right now you don't think? No? I thought not. But, as I say, it was just a courtesy call, on the off chance. …Well good to talk to you anyway … thanks for your time. Bye."

The problem here is that the prospect may well have had a storage problem that the caller could address. However, the cold caller was so intent (as they usually are) on dumping their scripted words on the prospect that the following happened:

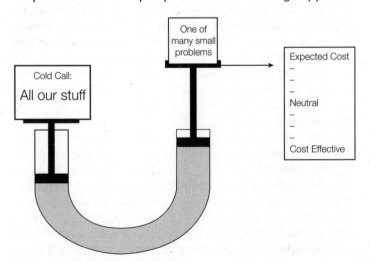

Once the cold caller began talking he didn't let up. Obeying the natural laws governing the operation of the average human brain, within 30 seconds of the start of the pitch, the prospective customer wasn't listening anymore. He wasn't the slightest bit engaged with the process. But, as the caller was still droning on with a lot of facts about his company, whatever it was he was selling was probably going to be expensive. There is a direct correlation between a seller talking about all his stuff and customers raising early cost objections.

The end result is typical of most cold calls and is highly predictable. The prospective customer knows the pitch has ended because there is no voice droning in his ear anymore. He is polite and well mannered, and may well have a vaguely irritating problem with storage that somebody mentioned to him the other day, so he routinely asks how much all this service costs. He definitely doesn't have enough of a problem at the moment to entertain the need for an appointment with the seller, so he asks for a brochure, and ... that's it.

The brochure when it arrives (indeed *if* it arrives [more on this later]) will join a pile of other brochures in the corner. The small problem will be subsumed by new problems and pushed further on to the backmost burner. The brochure will then inevitably go into the trash during spring cleaning. The caller won't ever call again ... "not a prospect"!

You will see from the diagram above, that the real cause of the problem is the weight of facts and features (the stuff) pitched by the cold caller. Far from addressing and expanding the potential customer's awareness of his specific, as yet "unadmitted" problem, he has totally ignored it. The caller believed, as do most sales people, that the art of selling is all about piling up all your good stuff, as quickly as possible, in front of the prospect. The prospect, so the theory goes, will then consider all that has been stacked up in front of him (in this case aurally) and select the bits he likes. After a little more discussion the deal will be done.

> "Ah ... the theory is great ... unfortunately it doesn't
> work like that."

The art of business persuasion, at any stage including a cold call is *not* in the telling, the gift of the gab, the presenting or the pitching.

Countless experiments and a huge amount of academic research show that people, customers, prospective customers (and remember that is sometimes you and me) are most persuaded when they persuade themselves. *The best way to persuade a prospective customer is to make sure that the prospective customer does most of the talking.* The true art and science of selling is *not in the confident "telling"* but in the *conversational "questioning"*.

In short the best sellers and cold callers do one thing differently. They...

Ask more questions!

The case for questions

I would like you to just stop for a moment and help me with a little experiment. And to do that I'd like to ask you a question.

That shirt or top you're wearing now ... where did you get it?

... Did you have a quick think? Do you remember exactly? Actually it doesn't matter that much where you got it. But what I would like you to do now, is think about exactly what happened between you and me just then. Straight out of the pages of this book I asked you a question … and immediately following that what did you have to do? You had to *think* didn't you? … Actually *you* had to think about what *I* wanted you to think about. That's the formidable power of questions. When you ask somebody a question it's like getting hold of their lapels and jerking them toward you. They are forced to think about what you want them to think about.

If you'll allow me to use a rather macabre illustration, a good torturer, for example, wouldn't need to touch you with his "no-anesthetic dental instruments." All he would have to do to get you to tell him where "the gold" is hidden is use your own imagination in his favor. "Are you going to tell me where you've hidden it?" he might ask, very pleasantly, as he uncovers his instruments, while you watch anxiously strapped securely into the chair. "No of course you're not … you're far too brave." He continues… "But what do you think it's going to be like tomorrow morning when I start to probe for some loose fillings in your mouth. Then begin to pull out some perfectly healthy teeth?" "Awful" you mumble. Your imagination is already working overtime. "Yes. 'Awful' is probably a good word in this context" he continues. "Anyway I will leave you now and pop back tomorrow to see whether you've changed your mind. If you don't mind I'll leave all these things here, where you can see them, ready for us to begin this time tomorrow. Goodbye for now." Now, be honest, when he returns tomorrow morning, after leaving you overnight to think things over, do you think you are going to tell him what he wants to know? You bet you are.

In the same way when we are selling ideas to people we are actually selling solutions to problems. But unless the prospect has started to think about the specific problem he has first and in some detail, there is only a small chance that he will ever think of buying your solution.

The only value you have to the prospective client is your possible ability to solve a problem. It is surprising to some trainee cold call chickens how much prospective customers are willing to tell you about their problems, when it appears that you are genuinely interested in hearing about them. When you encourage prospective customers to start talking by answering your questions—carefully planned questions—about problems you know you can solve, the diagram we looked at before moves in a different way. By taking time to prepare and then apply the "I.K.E.A." model (introduced earlier in the book) you will find that your cold calling:

● becomes more focused
● is targeted at prospective customers who typically have the sort of problem you can fix
● ensures that the prospective customer stays engaged with your call
● gives you a better chance that the potential customer will actually relate your questions to the potential problems he or she has

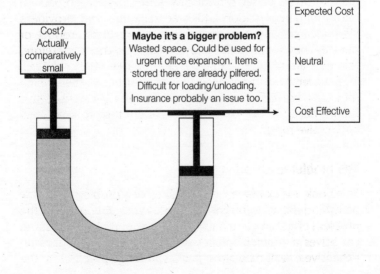

- minimizes the chance that he or she will raise objections and reject you
- give you a 20 times greater chance that you and the prospect will come away from the call with a satisfactory outcome.

So what questions are you going to ask the prospective customer when you make your cold call? How do you construct some questions that will get the customer to think about the problems he or she has—the problems you can fix?

The challenge here is for you to decide, right now, exactly what problem you are setting out to solve for the people who will become your customers. You have no other value than your ability to solve their problems. It doesn't matter what the product is. Because if it *sells* then it *is* solving a problem for somebody.

I am always surprised when I ask salespeople the question, "What problem(s) do you solve for your customers?" ... how many of them either cannot give a quick answer or launch into a long explanation which actually does not provide a clear idea of why existing customers use their product or service. They simply don't know. It is little wonder, therefore, that they are getting so many rejections when they cold call. They haven't got the slightest idea about the ways in which they can create value in the minds of their prospective clients, because they know nothing about the problems they could solve for them.

The problems we all solve

This book, for example, sets out to solve a problem you may be having initiating business opportunities. A cup solves the problem of getting liquid into you without making a mess. A car solves a problem of personal transport, and if it is an expensive one, it may also solve a self-image problem for the driver. Ask yourself what problem or problems wallpaper solves? What about a bank, printing company, cleaning service, water-cooler supplier, publisher? McDonalds compared with a high street café?

The thing to realize here is that the customers rarely buy what the product *is*. How it is made, the component parts, how many people work there and all its other so-called "features" are generally of passing interest. The real issue is: "What does (or could) the product or service do for me? What problem does it solve? What's in it for me?" Or, as Helena Rubenstein so memorably put it, "In the factories, we make 'make-up', but in the shops we sell hope."

The first thing to realize about your product or service is that it has three elements. These are its **Features**, its **Advantages** and its **Benefits**. Now, I can already hear many old selling hands start to yawn at this point, and quite understandably too. What is known as "Feature/Benefit" selling has been around since the 1960s. Yet the fact is, the majority of sales people come up with strange answers when asked to define each element and relate it to their own product. Most of the time they get it completely wrong. However, having a clear perception of these elements is 100% necessary before you can begin to plan the questions you are going to ask in your cold call.

Features

A so-called "feature" of a product is a raw fact about it. For instance, I am looking at a telephone on the desk in my study. Ten features I can tell you about it by simply looking at it are these.

- It is a telephone which allows me to talk to people.
- It has 12 major push keys with numbers printed on them.
- It has five silver function keys.

- It has a loudspeaker function.
- It has an LCD display panel.
- It has a rounded design.
- It is made of black plastic.
- It stores up to 100 numbers in its memory.
- It has 5 different ring-tones.
- It is cordless.

Each one of those points is a raw fact about the telephone. If somebody wanted to sell that phone to me, or anyone else, they would be well advised to prepare an answer to the burning question against each one: "So what?"

Each one of those features is only of use as a selling point if I (the potential customer) recognize the problem I would have if it was not there. It is no use, either, expecting the customer to make the automatic connection between the visible feature and the way it would help solve a problem. You the seller have to do it for them. It's not because people are thick, it is because they are lazy.

So, if you have a product or service in mind, right now, that you would like to start to cold call about as soon as possible, start by taking these immediate steps.

1. Get yourself a sheet of writing paper.
2. Turn it into a landscape position.
3. Divide it into three columns with a pen and head the first left-hand column "Features."
4. List the 10 top features or raw facts about that product.

Just like this:

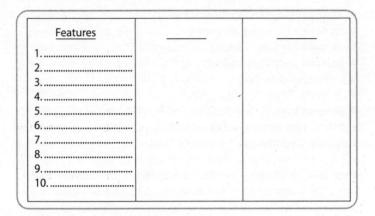

Features	_____	_____
1...................................		
2...................................		
3...................................		
4...................................		
5...................................		
6...................................		
7...................................		
8...................................		
9...................................		
10.................................		

Once you've done that your next step is to move to the second column across and head it up "Advantages." Each one of the features you placed in the first column will have one or more possible "advantages" connected with it. Advantages are "potential benefits" and Benefits are simply solutions to explicitly admitted problems. An "advantage" only turns into a "benefit" if the prospective customer has admitted to himself (or herself) the true extent of a problem with all its knock-on effects (the "K" in I.K.E.A.) It is a rare problem that stands alone and affects nothing else in an organization.

The simplest way to turn a feature into its component advantages is to ask any existing users of your product/service what life would be like without it. With any brand new or, as yet, unmarketed product you just have to imagine that you are in front of a potential customer and have just shown him one of your features. The imaginary customer looks blank and says, "Yeah ... so what?" It is now your job to describe to the prospective customer the type of typical problem fixed by that feature.

Remember, also, that the key motivators that drive any of us to do anything, can be divided into four groups; the so-called "Four **P**s": **P**ower, **P**rofit, **P**restige and **P**leasure. Each time you write an answer to the imagined "So What?" your answer must directly, or by implication, address one of these key motivators. Some definitions of these motivators may be useful here.

Power refers to anything that will enable the user to exercise control over events, work situations, people, and generally stay one step ahead of everyone else.

Profit is anything directly connected with money—either saving it, cutting costs, reducing expenditure or indeed making a profit. You may consider that profit is the prime objective of every commercial enterprize and yet, particularly for some wealthy individuals, it is merely a way of keeping score. The next motivator on the list "prestige" is far more important to many than profit.

Prestige concerns the type of honor or high opinion that is inspired by a high ranking, influential, or successful person. These people demand a Rolls Royce rather than a Mini, only want the best table at the restaurant, insist on only shopping at very exclusive establishments even for products that they could buy for a lot less elsewhere. Why? Because they can and they want everyone else to know that too! And finally …

Pleasure. This is anything to do with ease of use, an easier life, fun, enjoyment, eating, drinking, and being merry in general.

So you're ready now? Look at each feature, imagine the "So What?" and write your reply. For *example:*

Feature: This telephone has an LCD Display Panel.

Advantage: "When you receive an incoming call a glance at this panel, before you pick up the handset, will enable you to see which number is calling you and control which calls you answer and which you don't" (*the* **Power** *motivator*).

Remember there is very often more than one advantage connected with each feature. Go down the list and write down every one that comes to mind. Once you've done that, you can start on the most important task of all … preparing to construct some questions about problems you know you can solve.

Many people trained in the old ways of Feature/Benefit selling, as I was, simply got used to turning features into benefits and then throwing those at potential customers in a very enthusiastic manner and hoping for the best. What we called **benefits** back then were actually only potential benefits or what we now call **advantages**. We had none of the research-based techniques now available to 21st-century sellers. We were also trained in something called "probing" which was a very rough and ready form of questioning but was not as focused and sophisticated as the questioning techniques you are about to learn and apply.

Questioning skills, based on features, advantages, and benefits, are at the heart of all effective cold calling. However, the way we apply them varies according to the purpose of the call.

Now is the moment that you need to consider the purpose of your cold call. In your case is it:

A. To make an appointment to sell face-to-face ?

or

B. To sell a product or service directly over the phone?

The two objectives vary mainly in the types of question we ask. When cold calling to sell a product directly over the telephone you will find the type we call **concern questions** are most useful. On the other hand when cold calling to make a face-to-face appointment, you will find **commitment and consistency questions** are far more effective.

Cold calling to make an appointment

When I ask delegate audiences in our open seminars to tell me the objective of their cold calling, the most common answer I get is: "To make an appointment." So this is where we will begin.

Getting a prospective customer to agree to give you an appointment as a result of your cold call requires that you keep the I.K.E.A. model clear in your head. The prospective customer is not going to do it just because you sound like a nice person.

"Good morning Mr Prospect, my name is Joe Bloggins of Emergency Computer Associates. Could you tell me, are you the person who looks after all your computer servicing? ... Good well, we are local computer system repair experts and I was wondering whether I could make an appointment to come round and talk to you about how we might be of service to you?"

I get at least one cold call everyday like that from cold callers selling everything from stationery supplies to telephone services. What do you think I say to them? Correct: "No thanks we do it ourselves," "We already have a supplier that we're happy with," "We have no need," "We're too small" and all that old "baloney."

It's a fact that if you ask someone—a potential customer—to do something too quickly, or in the wrong way, or if they feel that you are going to endeavor to persuade them to do something, the answer is rather predictable. In any case, none of the I.K.E.A. rules has been followed. The poor cold caller is simply setting himself up for failure over and over again.

True, the occasional potential customer may, just at that moment, have experienced a computer failure and it may just be your good fortune to be the right person on the phone at the right time. But you can't count on it and definitely can't let that hit and miss approach dictate your cold call strategy. So let's apply some real psychological science to the process. Let us look at the science behind "brainwashing!"

Yes, brainwashing!! Far from being based on the old image of a naked, electric light bulb swinging hypnotically from the ceiling while you, deprived of sleep, are forced to listen to a relentless foreign voice intone some alien political mantra 24 hours a day ... it turns out that the process is far more subtle. It is also a process that cold call chickens can use to their own, significant advantage. It is based on the following fact: human beings, or more correctly human brains, like to be consistent.

It was discovered by the Korean army during the Korean war in the early 1950s, that if you could get a prisoner to first of all agree a few times that the room they were in had white walls, a wooden bed and table, and a yellow door (a true and undeniable statement of visible facts), subtly shifting one of the facts after a few days (e.g. that the walls are now cream colored) would be agreed without question by the prisoner. Over several more days of similar subtle changes it was quite possible to completely, by suggestion alone, get the prisoner to agree that the room (actually painted exactly the same as before), had a completely different color scheme.

Discovering this strange phenomenon enabled the army using the same techniques to, gradually, get a completely different and alien political ideology agreed by prisoners.

In a subsequent and similar experiment in the US a random group of car drivers in a Californian town were asked to display a very small sign in the rear window of their car which read "BE A SAFER DRIVER." After a few days the researchers returned with a much larger wooden placard designed for mounting on a frame to be erected on the driver's front lawns. This time it read "DRIVE WITH CARE" and the request to display it was also extended to drivers not asked to display the first small "back window" sign. This time the researchers came armed with a picture of a fine family home with a really grubby, mediocre version of the sign displayed on the front lawn—which almost hid the entire house from the road.

Over 80% of the people who had not been asked to display the first small sign refused to display the large sign, but over 75% of the drivers who had the first sign in their car windows agreed.

As an extension to this experiment the same residents were asked to sign a "Keep My California Beautiful" petition. A few weeks after that they were once again requested to place the large placard on their lawn and half of them agreed even though the primary request was different in both subject (Beautiful California) and action (signing the petition). It appeared, following further analysis of the results, that the first action altered the way in which the people saw themselves ("I'm a good and neighborly citizen") and that in turn caused them to act, the next time, in a way that reflected that.

So after that short explanation of the psychological science behind our actions, what has all this to do with making cold calls for an appointment an easier process?

Let me say right away that you are not going to become a brainwasher. But knowing how the human mind tends to work, is going to provide you with a simple and powerful tool for getting your prospective customer to say "yes."

Kids do it naturally

By the way, I only became aware of how susceptible I was to this very same process when my own daughter innocently used a simple version of it on me a few years ago. She had just passed her driving test and was coming to the end of her schooling before going on to university in the UK. There was to be a final school disco (no alcohol) and she was going to attend. About a week beforehand she asked whether, as a special treat I'd let her drive the family car there. With some trepidation and some confidence in the fact that there was to be no alcohol at the event I agreed. A few days later she knobbled me again: "You know you said I could borrow the car on Friday night?"

"Yes"

"Well I don't have much money so could you lend me some for some gas?"

"What? ... well I suppose so ... here you are. Go and fill it up"

On the Thursday night she went for the *coup de gras*. "Dad you know you said I could have the car on Friday night?"

"Yeeees"

"And you know you gave me some money for gas?"

"Yeeeeess"

"Well could I do one more thing? Could I stay at the disco until it finishes at 1am?!"

Now what had she done up until this point? She'd got a "yes" commitment to borrow the car. She'd then built on this and got a further "yes" commitment to money for gas.

The final request was built on two previous commitments so reinforced with this influence I said "yes" once again (and fortunately for all the event passed without a hitch!).

But consider this: do you think if one week before she had asked straight out: "Dad can I stay out until 1am next Friday?" I would have allowed it? Probably—almost definitely—not! Simply by building on each previous commitment, she got the "yes" she wanted, and that methodology is what we are going to apply to the core of the outline script for your cold call. We call all of this the **rule of consistency**. It is a close cousin to a second complimentary rule **the rule of commitment** and we will be using both of them later in our cold call script.

The rule of commitment is based on the fact that once a person has verbally committed to take some action, it is more than 80% probable that they will take that action. This theory was borne out in a number of experiments a few years ago, which included one in which a researcher was seen to be sunbathing on a crowded beach. After half an hour or so he got up and walked down to the sea for a swim leaving all his belongings, including a CD player on his towel. After a few minutes another researcher (playing the part of a thief) raced down the beach and on reaching the vacant towel "snatched" the CD player and ran off with it. Only about 4 of the 20 odd people sunbathing next to the vacant towel, did anything to stop the theft or remonstrate with the thief. The experiment was repeated a number of times with similar results. A day later the same sunbathing researcher was lying out on the sand in the same place but this time before going down to the water he asked local sunbathers if they would "watch his things." They all told him they would. This time when the "thief" ran by and snatched the CD player, nearly all the local people who had committed to guarding the sunbather's property tackled him and got the CD player back.

Another profession that makes good use of this human trait is the restaurant trade. One of the biggest problems for them is the potential customer who books a table then fails to show up. Restaurant owners have found they can counter this quite effectively by asking, before they end the booking call, "If you do have to cancel you will let us know won't you?" Over 80% of customers who commit to doing this will actually call in advance if they do have to cancel. When combined with the rule of **consistency** the rule of **commitment** makes a powerful tool for cold call chickens.

So armed with all the previous material we are ready to prepare an effective cold call script. On pages 124–126 is a three-section outline script designed for making cold calls which have the objective of getting an appointment. I don't want you to think in terms of "scripts" for cold calling. Such hardwired scripts always sound very false to the person being called. However, at this stage, it serves very well to illustrate how an effective call should be structured.

The first section of the script deals with the ways in which your first contact with the company (often a so-called gatekeeper) should be *diplomatically* handled. The second section is where you can see how to actually apply the consistency and commitment rules. The third section is an outline of an effective way to deal with any objections that you will inevitably come up against. It is well worth saying that if you apply good questioning technique combined with the I.K.E.A. model you will find that you have to deal with far fewer objections than with the hit and miss methodology applied by the vast army of average chicken cold callers.

But first a word about gatekeepers, secretaries, and personal assistants

Earlier in this book I mentioned the confrontational, even dismissive, ways in which 1960s trained sales people were told to deal with these important support staff. The ways we were trained in back then will not wash today. I admit that I don't particularly want to have to deal with gatekeepers and will avoid it if I can. They, in turn are trained professionals only doing their job protecting the senior influential people I need to be talking to. So here are some guidance notes to assist you in your dealings with them.

- First, there is no underhand methodology involved. When talking to them you must tell the truth and act profession- ally. Remembering the **I** and **K** in I.K.E.A., you must make absolutely certain that you have done as much **I**ntelligence gathering as you can before picking up the phone and that you have full **K**nowledge of the problem solving advantages of your product or service.

- The first person you are likely to encounter is the switch- board operator. Make your introduction clear and intelligible. Speak relatively slowly—this is not a race in order to dump words on the other side then run away.

  Tell the person exactly who you are and the name of your company and ask that person to connect you to the man- ager or director you want to speak to.

  That person should be the one who, your research shows, is most likely to be in charge of the key decisions connected with the proposition you intend to place before them.

  If you're still not sure, ask for the PA to the Managing Director or CEO. Chances are you will be connected with the person's PA but nevertheless, endeavor to get the per- son you really want to speak to first.

  If the switchboard person tells you they will connect you with the PA say, "OK, that's fine."

- "Good morning ... my name is *Joe Decipherable of Acme Widgets?*... Mr Head Honcho please. Thank you ... Oh that's fine I will speak to his PA ... by the way ... could you tell me that person's name please?" When the switch-board operator puts you through, say to the PA:

"Good morning my name is *Joe Decipherable of Acme Widgets*. Am I talking to *Jean Small, Mr Honcho's PA*?" (This of course depends on whether or not you have managed to get the PA's name.

If the person you are speaking to tells you they are not the PA ask if you can be passed to them. If it is the PA proceed as follows)

"I wonder if you can help me please?"

The person will normally say something like, "yes" or "I'll try ... what can I do for you?"

Your reply should then go something like this:

"I am very interested in getting some advice on how I should go about submitting a strategic proposition to your organization about the ways in which we could provide several advantages in the area of *your product or service's key area*."

(One note of caution here is not to go into too much detail or you will have the person saying: "Oh ... we do that ourselves in-house" or, "Actually we are quite happy with our existing supplier"). "... Can you tell me who I should talk to, first of all, who is in charge of this and what is the best way to go about it?" Alternatively you could ask: "Can you guide me to the best way of finding out who in your organization is in charge of strategy in the area of *your product or service's key area*."

- From here on, it's in your own hands. Now you have con-tact with the PA, take his/her guidance and act on it. Making sure you keep in step with this organization's way of doing things is very important. It is just about as important as the whole proposition you are going to put to them and you now have a potential ally to guide you.

- But I did say at the start of this section that I will always avoid getting involved with gatekeepers if it is at all possible and I recommend that you do the same. In this regard let me give you some guidance on times of day and conditions which make coming up against them less likely: gatekeepers tend not to be at their desks before 8:00am or after 6:15pm. The older gatekeepers are also, very often, not to be found at their desks at lunchtime. Many gatekeepers have kind bosses who allow them to go home early on Fridays, perhaps 4:45 pm onward. Bad weather (snow, hail etc.) is also a reason that gatekeepers are not at their desks. Weekends too … gatekeepers are rarely at their desks over the weekend.

The above, however, are all times and conditions during which their bosses (more often than not the very people you *really* want to talk to) ARE there and completely unguarded! *Carpe diem*!! Oh and by the way … if you are at this moment saying to me, "What? I'm not starting work that early in the morning … staying that late at night … working during weekends and all that. … No way!!" Then I have to remind you that selling is not a "9 to 5" activity. When selling you're not paid for the time you spend at your desk or in the office. As a professional seller and cold call chicken you are paid only what you're worth.

Weekend calls? What!

Here is a last, final, final point on this subject. Some people who attend our seminars challenge me on the advisability of phoning people during the weekends or outside normal business hours. "Don't they get upset?" they ask. Well I'll tell you what these senior decision makers often say when I call them at these unexpected times. "Mr Etherington … can you tell me how you got through to me?" ... so I tell them how I did it ... I tell them what I planned to do and how I executed the plan. Then they generally reply, "Really that's very interesting ... actually that shouldn't have happened. We'll have to tighten things up round here. But ... do you think you could you teach our salesforce to do precisely that?" It appears that most senior managers don't want to receive cold calls, yet absolutely expect their own salesforce to be doing it! Funny old World isn't it?

So now to the script. The one displayed on the next page is typical of the way I approach cold calling. It follows the model we have already discussed in this book but I am going to analyze it for you because there are yet more powerful and persuasive elements contained in it which we have not yet addressed. If you care to use it as a model just substitute your name, company name, and key product advantages for mine.

Script analysis

1. In the first line of the top block "A" you will notice the text reads:

> "Good morning. This is Bob Etherington of SpokenWord Ltd may I speak to Mr Head Honcho please. Thank you!"

What do you think makes this a particularly strong request? Read the whole line out loud to yourself . Do you notice anything? In particular the words, "Thank you" at the end. It is a strange fact that if you add these words to this or any similar request, it has the effect of changing a "request" into a "command." If you apply it you will find you are put through directly to the person you really want to speak to about 50% of the time. Is it infallible? No of course not ... it simply increases your chances of not getting caught up in a gatekeeper conversation.

2. In the lower section of the same top block you will see a reference to voicemail. You will be aware that these days you stand a very high chance of being put through to voicemail rather than being able to talk to a real person. And there is one key rule for the majority of voicemail messages. Keep it very short. This seems to be an impossible rule for many cold callers to master. As soon as the "beep" has sounded they start to talk and talk and talk. They leave almost their whole sales spiel on the answering machine. And what effect do you think this has? How many of those left messages are ever returned? The answer is, hardly any. Why should the prospect call you back? The full sales pitch is on the machine. Actually the prospect didn't listen to much of it because after less than half a minute the delete key was pressed. So what can be done? Simple ... when it's on voicemail keep it short and intriguing; VERY short.

Less is more

The best and most effective messages, which have a 90% chance of a call back are as simple as this: "Good morning Mr Prospect. My name is Bob Etherington. I wonder if you could give me a call please. My number is 020 7486 4008. Thank you Mr Prospect. Goodbye." The voice tone is kept slow, slightly deeper than my normal tone of voice and the words are spoken with a smile. It may sound daft but the reason for using these particular voice tone attributes is that they are associated, unconsciously by most listeners, with two important traits: power and authority. Powerful people have no reason to rush and are used to being listened to. You will find that a short, truthful voicemail, delivered and left in this way, is sufficiently provocative for most listeners, and that you are more or less guaranteed a call back. Even if this brings you no success there are yet more ways in which you can intrigue your intended audience and get a positive reaction. We will look at these in the final part of this book.

3. Now I would like you to look at the top of the middle block "B" of the script, at which stage I am assuming you have finally got through to the person you wish to talk to. Take a look at the top line in which you are introducing yourself to the prospective customer:

> *"Good Morning Mr Prospect my name is Bob Etherington of SpokenWord Ltd. Do you have a moment?"* or *(even better)* *"Can you talk?"*

It is always best to check that the person has time to talk before you start, but even better than asking "Do you have a moment?" take a look at the "even better" alternative. "Can you talk" is an absolutely wonderful "initial-attention-grabber" for quite an interesting reason. It is a phrase which headhunters and recruitment consultants often use to check that the target person they would like to speak to is actually free to talk about a prospective job offer. So when most executives hear this phrase they start to behave like one of Pavlov's dogs without quite realizing why. Somewhere deep in their psyche they know, without anyone telling them, that this could be the "big-one." You therefore, just for the moment, have their undivided attention. The most common sound you will hear at this point, is the sound of a conversation being terminated at the other end and an office door slamming followed by a question: "Yes what can I do for you?"

Now you're quite safe. You have not told a single untruth so far. All you have done is introduce yourself and ask if the prospect can talk. The fact that you have employed a particular bit of insider-knowledge to get the person's attention is completely above board. The next phase is to capitalize on the fact that you have the person's attention and begin the process of obtaining the appointment you desire.

4. Stay in the middle block "B" of the script and consider the next sentence. Now that you have the prospective customer's attention you need to say something which will retain it and build on it. If you recall the I.K.E.A. model you will remember that the **E** stands for expansion. It is at this point that you need to expand your message by mentioning something that has a direct connection with the customer's business and links it to an advantage that you can offer. In this case:

> *"I saw the article about your expansion plans in the Financial Times this week. That is quite a challenging goal you have set. We are the professional training organization which is currently showing companies how to sell twice as much in the current tough markets and how to do it in the next 12 weeks."*

The message should be an absolutely truthful, provable, description of your abilities as a business and yet provocative enough to get the prospective customer to say something like, "Oh yes ... how are you going to do that?" This is the signal to move on to the next stage in which you begin to ask the series of planned "consistency and commitment" questions designed to arrive at the go-ahead for the appointment you desire. So at this point I will generally say: "Well do you mind if I ask you just a few questions first to see whether we can help you in this case?" and then, without pause move straight into the first of my planned questions.

5. Now the consistency and commitment process begins. Look at the questions numbered 1 to 7 in the middle block "B." Each one of these asks a question which is designed to lead to a verbal commitment that leads to the next question. Each question is subtly harder than the one before. Remember too, that I am using my own cold calling script as a model to illustrate various points. The one you prepare for your own business will be designed to address the advantages of yours.

Question 1. An easy no-brainer. I usually know the answer to this because I will have done my research (the **I** for Intelligence in I.K.E.A.). The object of asking the question is to get the prospect into the rhythm of answering the upcoming questions positively.

Question 2. A slightly harder question which I also know the answer to, designed to reinforce the rhythm started by question 1.

Question 3. Slightly harder again, and probing a little deeper this time. It is also designed to tell me whether I have to do any so-called "missionary work" for this account. "Missionary work" describes the extra task of having to prepare the ground for a sale before the sales process can even begin. In my world of business consultancy, for example, if I have discovered as a result of asking this question, that the use of business consultants is not common for this company, I would know that a fair amount of additional time would have to be spent convincing them of the value of using an outside consultant. That is even before I started work selling the value of my own business. Do I want to spend my valuable time doing this? It generally depends on the prospect and my current work schedule.

Question 4. In the world of selling no sales manager is ever happy with the level of sales. Even though the answer is pretty sure to be negative and often accompanied by a wry laugh, the answer continues to reinforce the growing commitment.

Question 5. Generally gets the prospect saying "yes" again because most companies have used expert consultants or considered it at sometime.

Question 6. Having got the prospect to say "yes" to question 5, I now add an advanatge to a similar question which, this time, is directly connected with my own business.

Question 7. This is a bit of a "sucker" question because asking the person if they would like some more information implies that I will now "let them off the hook" and send them some details. It generally gets another positive answer which now brings the total to seven in a row. Psychologically the prospective customer is now prepared for the "nextstep" or "close."

Question 8. The final "close" question is a classic "alternative close" but loses no power because of that. It can be used by any seller at anytime during the sales process including the cold call. *"Could I make an appointment to get your opinion on whether you think we could help in your business? Either Monday at 11:40 or would Tuesday at 9.15 be better? [SHUT UP]* The "alternative close" makes use of another peculiarity of the human brain—that if you offer a brain a choice of two alternatives it will tend to take one of them. It is used in the retail trade a great deal: in a shoe store, for example, "How would you like to pay for these sir? ... Cash or credit card?" From the sales clerk's point of view it's not a case of whether or not you're going to buy the shoes, that decision has been made for you. People hate to make decisions and love it when they are made for them. Over 80% of customers at this point choose one of the alternatives. Auto dealerships use it too because they know how tough it is for you to make a decision to spend several thousands of pounds or dollars of your hard-earned money on a motor vehicle. So they also help you by making the decision for you. They do it by linking the choice to some minor point rather than the whole big shiny car. "Well which is it to be Sir ... the red one or the blue one?" or, "Would you like with or without the sun roof?" or, "Do you want it with the 18 inch or the 21 inch alloy wheels?" No, of course it is not *impossible* for the customer to say "neither" but you will find that if you ask the question in a chatty confident tone, most people will respond by taking one of the choices you offer. In your case you're using the same technique to simply "close" an appointment ... in the example given the choice is "Monday or Tuesday." By the way, if the person you're talking to does say "neither" then make sure you have another pair of alternative dates ready to offer them.

You will also notice something else about the times being suggested. Instead of being, say, the typical "11am" or "9am," on-the-hour timings, they are actually a bit off the hour. *"Either Monday at 11:**40** or would Tuesday at 9:**15** be better?"* This is not accidental. The way you offer appointment times is very important to the way the prospective customer perceives the probable length of time he or she will have to devote to you. If you offer 11:00am or 9:00am, the person on the other end will, subconciously, round up the time to the next hour.

On the other hand, suppose it was *you* receiving the cold call and you were offered a choice of 11:40 or 9:15? With only that bit of information how long might you assume the meeting would last? Most people tend to round up to the nearest hour and say in the first case "20 minutes" and in the second case "45 minutes." As the proposed time is a lot less than a full hour and most people break down their day into one-hour slots, it makes it easier for the called person to agree to see you. You haven't *said* how long the meeting might last and when you get in front of the prospective customer, your face-to-face skill is probably so powerful that the pair of you will be there for well over an hour! That bit is up to you. Your objective at this stage is simply to secure the appointment.

6. The final block of the script is the part marked "C" and concerns what happens when they still try to put you off. How do you handle objections? The first thing to emphasize here is that by tackling cold calling in the way

described so far in this book, you will actually hear far fewer objections. This is because you are focusing your whole approach not on who you are or what you are, but on potential customers who are more likely to have the type of problems you can solve. Still, you will get *some* objections and this section deals with the most effective way to deal with them. The first one as you can see is the classic "put-off" "*Can you send me a brochure?*" or, "*Could you outline all that in an email to me?*" or even, "*Tell me about it now....*" Too many cold callers hear that as a buying signal and enthusiastically send off the desired information or go into "telling" overdrive, then sit back and wait for the return call—"we'll let you know" mode. Sadly it rarely comes and the prospect was just being polite. It is what we call a continuum (con-tin-you-um)—in this case it describes a vacuous request going nowhere. It has no built-in commitment from the prospective customer. So the first action you must take, on hearing those words, is to politely counter them with an alternative suggestion and immediately re-request the appointment with the identical alternative close again: "*Yes, Mr Prospect that is why I would like to meet you. To give you the information you are interested in and avoid wasting your time. I have my diary here so which would be better for you Monday at 9:40am or Tuesday at 11:15?*" **Do not listen to all the cynical, negative, and blame-culture people in your office (the kitchen and drinks machine brigade**—look back at page 29!) **who will inevitably tell you that this determined approach won't work**. When I am cold called I always test the mettle of the caller by throwing up a few random objections to see whether they collapse (80% of them do indeed fall at this first hurdle) or keep going as they should. Those latter ones are the ones who get the appointments.

Be one of those. If the prospect doesn't give in and still insists on seeing a brochure or something in writing first, you have another strong card to play; now is the time to apply the "commitment" part of the rules for consistency and commitment. So when the prospect insists on the brochure you say with a slightly mischievous laugh in your voice, *"OK, sure Mr Prospect ... but if I send you the brochure (or letter or email) you will definitely read it won't you?"* Then listen very carefully to the manner of the reply. If the person on the other end confidently says, "Yes I certainly will." Then you can be pretty confident yourself that it will be read; maybe not every word and in detail but, having given you the verbal commitment, they will have developed a mental drive to carry out their commitment.

If, on the other hand, the person sounds a lot less committed to reading it and says something along the lines of, *"Yes well, OK ... I probably will ... if I get time."* Then you need a total change of approach. There is clearly no verbal commitment here, so you need to move on to more lucrative ground as soon as possible. In such cases I always adopt the point of view that it is probably a "no" for now but may also be a "yes" tomorrow (nothing stays the same after all) and I say something like this, *"OK, I'll tell you what Mr Prospect. I can see that this isn't a particularly important issue for you at the moment and I don't want to fill up your in-tray (or incoming mail folder) with a load of 'bumph!' I'll keep your name on file if I may and call you again in about 6 weeks or so. How does that sound?"* Prospects are often very surprised at this non-pushy approach and agree that a later call would be preferable. All you have to do now is keep a note in your diary of the date you said you would call back and then do it. Remember that steady persistence is the way to succeed with most things in life. Most people don't persist—so be the one who does.

Another common objection is, *"I'm not really interested"* or , *"Actually we do it all ourselves"* or even, *"We used to use a company like yours and it was useless."* When you hear this type of objection a little more cunning is required. One very effective way of handling it is by being completely illogical with your reply. Your best bet is to say, *"Yes Mr Prospect and that is exactly why we should meet. I only need 10 minutes of your time. If you're not convinced after 10 minutes I will leave. So when's the best time for you? Next....etc. etc.?"* Your reply makes little sense in the light of what the person has just told you and you will often hear them hesitate for a minute, a little confused, *"er what...?."* *"What is the best date in your diary for us to meet?"* You will be surprised how often, in this moment of trying to connect the logical or illogical steps that have just taken place, how often the person will agree to see you.

Finally in the line of common objections, are those concerned with immediate "lack of budget" or "cost." Here your answer is quite straightforward. Simply be honest but at the same time carry on being politely persistent. *"I appreciate that Mr Prospect. At this stage it is important that we meet so that we can discuss your future needs regarding our service. Have you got your diary handy? I can meet you on _____day at __:40 or _____day at __:15."*

All these objections are very common and you will often have to deal with more than one of them in a single call. As a rule-of-thumb you should be prepared to hear and handle at least four such objections in any one phone call. After that you have too much to do to plug away at that particular prospect so give in gracefully, politely terminate the call and move on to the next one.

Power script for an appointment

(A)

You: Good morning. This is *Bob Etherington* of *SpokenWord Ltd.* may I speak to *Mr Head Honcho* please ... Thank you! ... Oh that's fine I will speak to his PA then ... oh by the way, could you tell me the person's name please? Thanks.

You: (You're put through) Good morning this is *Bob Etherington* of *SpokenWord Ltd.* is that ... *Name*? are you the PA for *Director's name* I wonder if you could help me please? I wonder if you can help me please? I am very interested in getting some advice on how I should go about submitting a strategic proposition to your organization about the ways in which we could provide several services *designed to double the effectiveness of your sales force in the next 10 weeks.*

OR

You: Can you guide me to the best way of finding out who in your organization is in charge of strategy in the area of *sales and marketing*?

If sent straight to the Director's voice mail

You: Good morning Mr/Ms ⟨*Director's name*⟩. This is *Bob Etherington* of *SpokenWord Ltd. 0207 4000 7000.* I have an issue about your sales team which I would like to discuss with you. Would you please give me a call at _____. Thank you Mr/Ms ⟨*Director's name*⟩.

You're through NOW what?

B

You: Good morning Mr/Ms *(Director's name)*. My name is *Bob Etherington* of *SpokenWord Ltd.* Do you have a moment?

Prospect: Yes (If "no" ask when would be convenient)

You: **Can you talk?** I saw the article about you in the FT this week. That is quite a challenging goal you have set. We are the professional training organization which is currently showing companies how to sell twice as much in the current tough markets.

Prospect: Oh yes, how are you going to do that then?

You: Well would you mind if I asked you a few quick questions?

1. Could you tell me, do you have a large salesforce?
2. Am I correct in thinking that you are responsible for it?
3. Do you do all your own sales training in house?
4. Are you currently completely happy with your level of sales?
5. Have you ever considered using a consultant to help improve results in any area?
6. Would you consider using a company like SpokenWord if we could show you the ways in which we can help bring in more business for you?
7. Would you like some information about SpokenWord and what we do?
8. Could I make an appointment to get your opinion on whether you think we could help in your business? Either _____day __:40 or would _____day at __:15 be better? (SHUT UP)

(If the prospect says "neither" have two other alternatives ready PERSIST—"no" is NOT forever)

Getting through objections. delays and other things

C

Prospect: Send me a brochure.

You: That is why I want to see you—so I can give you the information you are interested in and avoid wasting your time. I have my diary here; would next — —day or next — —day be better?

Prospect: I really want to see a brochure first.

You: If I send you a brochure ... will you *definitely* read it?

Prospect: Yes (positive sounding—ask for address)

Prospect: Yes ... OK ... (sounding vague)

You: Mr Prospect as I don't think you are really interested at the moment I won't add to your junk mail this time but I will send you my card and keep in touch every few months. (Confirm address)

Prospect: I am not really interested / I have a similar service already / You're wasting your time.

You: Exactly why I only want 10 minutes of your time. If you're not interested after 10 minutes. I will go. Would _____day or _____day be better?

Prospect: I don't have any budget left / We can't afford anything else.

You: I appreciate that. At this stage it is important that we meet so that we can discuss your future needs regarding our training. Have you got your diary handy? I can meet you on _____day at __:40 or _____day at __:15?

Cold calling to sell a product directly over the telephone

We recently changed the supplier of stationery items for the training company owned by my business partner and myself. It was as a result of a cold call—in fact a series of cold calls— and eventually I gave in. I have never met the lady cold caller in question and probably never will. I had never heard of her company before. The process the young lady used could have come straight out of the pages of this book. Maybe that is why I eventually gave her the business. She did it so well that I am going to use her approach as the final example for this part of the book.

Her initial opening and getting past our own gatekeeper tactics were excellent. However, our gatekeeping policy is quite strict because our time is so precious, and during the day we rarely have time to answer a lot of cold calls. She eventually got hold of me by calling on a Saturday morning as I was strolling round Hyde Park in London. We had actually spoken at least five times in the previous 12 months but I had always put her off with a range of spurious objections mostly on the theme "I *really* don't have time to talk right now." She was always polite but always persisted (just like it says in this book) and whatever I said or however grumpy I was, she always came back again. It must have been clear to her after several months that a different approach was needed—in her case the weekend-call strategy—and it worked. So, having won my attention, how did she proceed? Her approach was centered on "concern questions" which are based on product advantages.

When selling a product or service directly over the telephone you have to get the prospective customer thinking about the concerns he or she has which are related to their current way of doing business. Rather than using the consistency and commitment rules, a more powerful approach is to work on the prospect's mental pain threshold.

The opening and objection handling sections outlined in the previous script remain untouched. But the center section, *"You're through NOW what?"* needs to be handled in a different way in order to have the greatest chance of success. The various diagrams on pages 93, 94 and 98 give you a good idea of the things NOT to do and the process necessary to create, in the prospect's mind, a feeling of urgency/need for the cold caller's solution.

Concern questions

So-called "concern questions" are carefully crafted questions designed to get the prospective customer to think about the problem the caller's solution could address. To begin to compile these seemingly innocuous but very powerful questions for your own product or service, you will first have to look again at the list of advantages you have written down for your product or service in the second column of the "Feature/Advantage" sheet of paper you prepared earlier.

Each one of these advantages is a potential solution to a problem but it means little unless the problem has first of all been uncovered and verified. The question compilation procedure I am going to suggest is rather like the American TV Quiz game *Jeopardy*. If you've never watched this show let me explain:

Jeopardy is a quiz in reverse.

The contestant is given the answer by the quizmaster and then has to think what the question might be that generated that answer. Therefore the quizmaster might say to the contestant: *"The River Thames."* To which the correct contestant reply would be: *"What is the river that flows through London?"*

BINGO!

This is exactly what I am going to get you to do now. So, look at the first advantage you've written down and think what question you could ask for which that advantage would be a solution. In my earlier telephone example I had, as an advantage: *"When you receive an incoming call, a glance at this panel, before you pick up the handset, will enable you to see which number is calling you and control which calls you answer and which you don't."*

So, if I was trying to sell you the telephone, my concern question might be: *"Mr Prospect you've told me you manage a very busy office here, can I ask how much of a headache it is to accidentally pick up time-wasting telephone calls because you are unable to screen them?"*

I've purposely picked a very simple example above, but no matter what the product or service you're endeavoring to sell, the concern question should have one particular attribute: it should not be particularly happy! A good concern question contains words like problem, pain, headache, costly, worry, dire, rough, complicated, delay, loss and so on.

In order to assist you a bit with this I have prepared some concern question prefixes which you can modify and adapt for your own use:

- "Are there any current *issues* with … ?"
- "Have you ever had any *difficulty* with … ?"
- "How much of a *problem* have you found … ?"
- "How does this sort of *crisis* effect … ?"
- "Have you every looked at the *risks* inherent in … ?"

- "Is it *difficult* to manage this level of *uncertainty* in … ?"
- "How much *hassle* does this cause when … ?"
- "What are the *costs* to your company associated with … ?"
- "Could not fixing this be *expensive* for you … ?"
- "What sort of *worries* do you have about … ?"
- "How *upsetting* have you found … ?"
- "What level of *panic* does this cause when … ?"
- "How *painful* has it been … ?"
  —"How *unpleasant* … ?"
  —"Does it make you *miserable* when … ?"
  —"Have you found it *time-consuming* when … ?"
  —"How much of a *nightmare* … ?"
  —"Does it cause you much *concern* when … ?"

The young lady cold caller who contacted me about stationery supplies used a lot of Concern Questions. I didn't bite on all of them but this is how she, very effectively, conducted the cold call. The names have been changed so that she doesn't get too embarrassed!

Her: Mr Etherington this is Molly Changename of Other Stationery Supplies. I was just looking at your website. I see your company offers various cold calling seminars.

Me: Yes that's right how can I help you? (Thinking: A prospective customer. I'd better listen)

Her: Do you run any other sales courses?

Me: Yes we do what are you particularly interested in?

Her: Well all of them really. How many do you run altogether every year?

Me: About 200 in all. We cover everything from cold calling to negotiating and public speaking.

Her: Really that's very interesting. You must use a lot of stationery products from paper and pens to printers and white boards. The reason I mention it is that at Other Stationery Supplies we offer a free, country-wide, same-day delivery service on every stationery item you can think of, and on all orders received before 12 noon.

Me: Oh yes, how do you do that? We're not a particularly huge organization ... yet!

Her: *OK, I realize that but could I just ask you a few questions? Have you ever made the mistake of running out of essential stationery items at the last minute?*

Me: Oh yes, we try very hard to avoid it but it has happened.

Her: *How much of a problem is it when you run out of things?*

Me: I think it could make us look very unprofessional. We don't like that at all!

Her: *Yes I can see what you mean ... when did it last go wrong like that?*

Me: We nearly ran out of covers for some specially prepared seminar Work Books recently. It was touch and go and I managed to find some by spending a great deal of my own time rushing around the West End of London. It was too late in the day to organize a delivery from our regular supplier. A real headache!

Her: *What about printer cartridges ... do you find them very costly at the moment?*

Me: They certainly are. We are constantly searching for cheaper ways of getting our printing done. But brand-name printer cartridges seem to be the one item that it's almost impossible to get a reduced price on.

Her: *Yes I know ... I expect you have the same problem with franking machine ribbons too.*

Me: Oh don't mention those. I usually get them from *a well-known large national manufacturer*. They offer a 48-hour service. Last time I ordered they didn't arrive on time, then when a box did arrive it contained a completely different product for a completely different customer. Then they promised to sort the mess out by the next day but delivered them to our old address. I eventually received them after 21 days ... and so expensive for what they are! I don't want to spend any time thinking about these piddling things—but I have to!

She continued asking questions like this, in a very conversational manner, for about 5 minutes. The thing was, I *knew* what she was doing but I discovered there was something very therapeutic in being asked about a typical work problem and have somebody listen.

When she had exhausted her list of concern questions she summarized what I had told her about my problems. She didn't mention any solution. It was just a summary of my moans over the previous 5 minutes. However, hearing her repeat them made me realize the true amount of time and money I could well be spending every month dealing with something as simple and stupid as paper, pens, and cartridges but very necessary for the correct functioning of this business. Then she said ...

Her: *Mr Etherington. I'd like to ask you a question. What difference would it make to you if all those stationery supply problems could be solved by my company? What would your life be like?*

Me: For a start, *if* you could wave that magic wand I wouldn't have to worry about stupid emergencies like going out to find book covers for half a day. The cost of our color printing supplies would be cut drastically, and our mail marketing campaigns would always be predictable and go out properly franked and on time ... only half our Christmas cards went out because of that last year! If that lot could be fixed it would be great!

Her: *Well I'm pleased to be able to tell you that Other Stationery Supplies can, first of all, offer you guaranteed, same-day delivery on absolutely any quantity of any item in our catalog—including book covers—provided you call us before midday. You also mentioned the problems you had with printers and franking machines. We are official suppliers of all accessories for all makes of printer and franking machine and offer the same-day service on these items too, and at a minimum of 25% less than any other supplier. We can offer you a list of our existing customers too, and we welcome you talking to any of them in order to satisfy yourself that they all get their orders on time and none of them has ever had to wait 21 days for ribbons. Mr Etherington we would like to become your stationery suppliers. What order would you like to place with us right now?*

So, standing there in Hyde Park, on a Saturday morning, I ordered 4000 sets of book covers (4000 fronts and 4000 backs), 20 sets of cartridges (tricolor and black) and several thousand binding wires. We've never looked back, her company is our main stationery supplier, they are very reliable and the prices are great!

But let us for a moment analyze her strategic approach to cold calling through which she, successfully in this case, was able to secure a new customer over the telephone.

First of all she prepared in the correct way. She obtained her **I** Intelligence, and took the trouble to find out a bit about the target company and what we did before she picked up the telephone. She was also very clear about the advantages her company could offer a potential customer. She had thought about the **K** Knock-on effects that a failure in stationery supplies could lead to and guided my thoughts, through her questions, down that road. She helped me **E** Expand her message in my mind. She also quickly ascertained in doing this, that I was a long-term customer of another supplier and therefore probably had experienced a lot of complacency (true) and adjusted an **A** Appropriate approach to fit where I was on the buying ladder. If I had told her that I had only just changed to a new supplier and had no cause to complain about them at that point, her message would have to be crafted differently and spread over several more months if she was ever going to succeed.

When she was finally ready to pick up the telephone and call us she discovered that our gatekeeper was difficult to get past. When she did get past the gatekeeper and get through to a decision maker (myself or my business partner) we were often "too busy" to talk to her. She clearly saw, however, that we were a good prospect for her business so she didn't give up. She persisted. In all she made five calls before getting lucky on the sixth and her unusual persistence meant that by the time we eventually got to speak to each other her name and company were familiar to me. Human beings are more willing to accept things into their lives that have a familiar ring to them.

When she finally got hold of me she opened the call in a way that clearly got my attention. She had been to our website and asked about something directly connected with my current business activities. She then proceeded, through a series of chatty "concern questions" to build my awareness of the fact that a small problem was in fact causing a lot of other problems. Not all her questions were relevant to me but on reflection I was doing most of the talking; she was nudging my thoughts down the right path with questions alone. She didn't try to persuade me by telling me anything. The persuading I was doing to myself. At the end she summarized what I had said using my own words to describe the situation. Then she asked me to describe what my business life would be like if my aggravating situation could be resolved. In the very act of telling her I was actually stating, in my own mind, the true benefits of changing my stationery supplier. I was then set up to listen to her confirm that she was able to match each one of the benefits I had stated.

On reflection I realized that most of the call had been based on her own investigative questions. I didn't feel at all interrogated though. It felt as if I had just had a pleasant conversation with someone who was interested in my problems.

I did not feel as if I had been "sold to." I felt as if I had "bought."

SECTION 5

A satisfied customer! We should have him stuffed.

BASIL FAWLTY – FAWLTY TOWERS BBC COMEDY SERIES 1975

How to keep them delivering the golden eggs

> "It is 90% easier to sell more things to an existing happy client than to go out and find a new one."

Cold calling, just like all the other aspects of selling, is simple ... it just isn't easy. For this reason we Cold Call Chickens need to find as many ways as possible to make our business lives as easy as we possibly can. So let me ask you this: would you prefer to *cold call* or *warm call*?

By cold call I mean a call you make, from scratch, to a prospective customer who has never done business with you before. Or one who has not given you any business for a very long time. On the other hand when I say *warm call*, I mean a sales call to a customer who has recently given you some business, which you delivered satisfactorily and with which that customer was at least satisfied or hopefully very pleased. Clients, who are happy with what you have provided in the recent past, are generally 90% easier to sell to, and it is 90% cheaper to get more business from them. Not only that, but if you can cut, by just **10%**, the rate at which regular customers in your existing customer base drift away from you, you can increase the profitability of your business by between **25%** and **90%**!

It is so very expensive to locate and bring on board a single, new customer, that every business worth its salt needs to devise and implement a program to keep existing customers in place. Your biggest enemy is your own complacency; an attitude which assumes that because an existing customer used your services recently they will automatically return to you next time they need something you provide.

This is not the case. If you are complacent you will, in effect, be leaving your back door wide open and competitors (like me) will stream in.

The biggest reason that your existing customers drift away from you is simple—they simply forget about you.

As a reluctant cold caller who now appreciates why, nevertheless, it must be done, you need to formulate your plan to keep your customers close by. You must keep your name familiar to them ... to make it easier to get more business from them ... to increase the amount of profit you generate ... to minimize the amount of cold calling you have to do you chicken!

This is what the majority of TV advertising is all about; reinforcing the familiarity of the product's name. If it is good enough for the big multinational makers of breakfast cereals, cars and washing powders, it is good enough for you too.

This is where I want to introduce you to something very simple I read about on the Internet five years ago, and which we have successfully applied to our own business in the past few years. It is a way of keeping existing customers close to you. It was apparently thought up by one of the world's top car sales people many years ago, who even made it to the *Guiness Book of World Records* because he was such a highly successful sales person. It is a system called a "Stay Close Program." It is not difficult to set up and it usually provides remarkable results if you apply it consistently. The original programs in the US were very simple but worked well.

All that is necessary is for you to design a very simple post-card and send it out.

The original stay close program cards had a simple message across the front which read, "We Like You!" Underneath that phrase, was the name of the company, their logo and their telephone number. On the reverse the name and address of the customer and space for the stamp. That was it.

Over 10,000 of these cards were sent out every week. Each month every current and past customer would receive an identical postcard. Remarkable as it may seem the results were spectacular. Sales kept pouring in just because the company worked on keeping their name familiar to the customers.

It is a simple idea. Maybe you think it is too simple—but think it through for a moment. If you were going to make a purchase and you had a mental list of, say, six or seven potential suppliers, who would you go to first? The less familiar "number five" on the list or the ones near the top? What about if your existing supplier isn't doing a particularly brilliant job but the number two supplier on your list has been making itself known to you on a regular basis?

This tendency for us to be attracted to familiar things which we are regularly exposed to was the subject of a university experiment a few years ago. A test group was apparently shown a sheet of white paper which was covered in 50 or so small designs made up of wiggly lines, circles, triangles and squares. They were allowed to look at it for half an hour after which time it was taken away. The next day each person in the group was shown a similar sheet covered with similar little designs. They were asked to mark the designs that had also been shown to them on the sheet they had seen the previous day. Most of the people in the group were unable to do this.

Then the group was asked to do something a little different. They were asked to place a mark against the wiggly-line etc. designs that they preferred. Most people chose the designs they had seen the day before. They couldn't say why ... they just "preferred" them.

It may seem to you, depending on which part of the world you live in, that a card emblazoned with the inscription, "We Like You" is just a little too simplistic. In cynical old Europe and especially the cynical old UK many of you may be curled up in paroxysms of derision at the idea that such a simple "sugary" message could have any effect at all. In this case you might be interested in the modification of the idea which we use very successfully in the UK and Northern Europe to keep our own regular clients close and our name familiar to prospective clients. Just by sending out similar cards to the ones just described on a regular basis, we obtain an enormous amount of both repeat and new business.

Instead of "We Like You," the front of our card displays an appropriate business cartoon. You can find these in great abundance on the Internet. Our favourites sites are www.cartoonbank.com and www.library.kent.ac.uk/cartoons. On these websites you can search for cartoons by subject or topic and gain access to the work of some of the world's top cartoonists. To license and download a particular high quality image costs remarkably little. For example, a license for up to 10,000 imprints generally costs about $250 (around

£150). We know the cards are unusual and we also know, because we have seen them, that they are pinned up on notice boards and stuck to the front of diaries.

The format of the card is always the same for branding purposes. The only thing that changes is the cartoon. On the front, below the cartoon, in a ½-inch (1cm) wide banner and always in the same corporate color and font, we show our website address and list three bullets about what we do. On the reverse a very short A.I.D.A. based message: a headline for **A**ttention, something provocative to hold their **I**nterest, **D**esire created by outlining the current seminar we're promoting and **A**ction initiated by telling them what to do to book their place … all in no more than about 25–35 words. Does it work and do they remember us? You bet. And you can do the same—you just have to do it.

In an age when everyone is trying to use both email and the web to promote their business and so much of it automatically becomes instantly deleted or "spam" mail, focused use of surface mail can be extremely useful to us cold callers. Apart from using it for our Stay Close program we also use it to open difficult doors. However, let me emphasize immediately that sending out mail shots and sales letters is NOT an easy substitute for picking up the telephone and making a cold call.

Sales letters in particular are very difficult to write. Even when written by highly skilled professionals and sent out in blanket mailings of several hundred thousand or more, they achieve a hit rate of between 1% and 2%, and that's just getting the recipient to open the envelope! So there is probably not much chance for you, as an amateur, to do any better.

What you *can* use snail-mail for, other than the Stay Close program postcards, is to open doors which appear to be firmly closed to you. When you have nothing to lose, therefore, you may want to try one of these suggestions (in our company we use all of them occasionally to great effect).

The first rule of mailing (other than postcards): *send something lumpy!* The reason for this is even more simple than, "the package looks interesting." It is that, if you make the package "lumpy" in some way, it is very difficult to place other mail on top of it, so it goes to the top of the pile!

Some of the lumpy things we place in the envelope to get attention (the A of A.I.D.A. again) are these:

A "screwed-up" mailer, brochure or flyer. If we send someone some advertising material "on-spec," we often crumple it up as much as we can before placing it in the envelope. Before sealing it up we also stick a small "Post-it" note on the crumpled up document bearing the legend:

Pre–crumpled for your wastepaper bin.

When we call, no more than 48 hours later (we *always* follow up with a telephone call) we find that 80% of the recipients have opened it, have remembered it and found it, if not hilarious, mildly amusing. We also find that as soon as we give our name to the PA we get the reaction, "*Oh yes you're the people that sent us that screwed-up flyer aren't you? Just a minute I'll put you through.*" As a result we are able to close selling appointments with them in about 80% of cases.

Another lumpy package can be created by first recording a simple message on an old-fashioned cassette tape:

> "*Good morning Mr Prospect. My name is .... of .... Company. I have been trying to make contact with you for several days. I know this is an unconventional approach but could you call me back please when you have a moment. My number is 020 7xxx xxxx. Thank you Mr Prospect.*"

I then handwrite the following message on a small label which I stick to the cassette. There is nothing else on it to indicate the identity of the sender:

Please play this tape as soon as possible.

Recipients find this just as intriguing and memorable as the crumpled flyer. It has a "Mission Impossible" quality. We also follow these up within 48 hours if we haven't heard from them and again get a great response.

A third idea which we have found very effective and "lumpy" can be generated by going to your nearest pharmacy or footwear supplier and getting some cheap shoe insoles; the sort of padded affair that cushions your feet or prevents bunions! We punch a small hole in one end and thread a rubber band through the hole, attached to one of our business cards. Across the back of the card is written:

> *Just trying to get my foot in the door.*

Once again, this gets noticed in a pile of boring junk mail. We do get business from it, so be careful of dismissing this or any of the other ideas as too "cheesy" for your "high class" business. We use all of these techniques and as a result take a lot of "high class" business from our own "high class" competitors.

One final emergency door-opener you may want to consider can only really be used by the females on your cold call team who have been endeavoring to contact a male prospect. First ask a playing card company to make you up a special order of playing cards: a pack of Aces of Hearts, a pack of Jacks of Hearts and a pack of Kings of Hearts.

When you receive your cards place a single Ace of Hearts, nothing else, in a plain white envelope and send it to the person you have been trying to speak to. The next day send the same person a single Jack of Hearts. The following day send a single King of Hearts. After a couple more days have elapsed make your cold call to the prospect. When the gatekeeper asks who is calling say simply, "Would you tell him it's the 'Queen of Hearts' please. Thanks." There is hardly a man alive who will not be intrigued and curious enough not to take your call. Again we have used and still use this door-opener to great effect.

Don't be a dumb chicken

For 95% of sellers the cold call is the very worst thing they can imagine. When they die and find they are not fortunate enough to get into Heaven, they believe Hell will be an eternity of cold calling. But as 85% of all new business in every market goes to the 5% of sellers who do cold call regularly, then it must be done in order for you to get the house in France, the Bentley, the ocean-going yacht, the helicopter and the huge bank balance.

Cold Calling for Chickens is really for the majority of sales people in every market; they are all just as chicken as you but you've had the courage to take the first step toward doing something about it by buying this book. There are some absolute certainties when making a cold call:

1. No prospective customer is waiting by the phone for your call.
2. Most prospective customers will have just as good a life without the service or product you provide.
3. Most prospective customers don't really want the hassle of changing the way they do things at present.
4. Not a single prospective customer cares about the raw facts and features of your product, however fancy or new they may be.
5. Unless, during the call, you can sow a little FUD (fear, uncertainty, and doubt) in the mind of your prospective customer, by asking effective questions in areas where you know you have a solution, you simply will not get either an appointment or a sale.

6. You must never assume before you pick up the telephone that the person you want to call is going to be grumpy, miserable or not a prospect. If you have done your I.K.E.A. work that person is a qualified prospect who can make use of your product and make a decision to buy.

To create value in the mind of your customer, ask questions that force the person to think about their problems. The best cold call callers are just as chicken as you. They simply ask more questions and persist. It's really as simple as that.

I look forward to hearing of your success.

About the author

Bob Etherington has been developing his reputation for sales success since the 1970s, in a career that has spanned many key global markets.

Having begun his sales career in 1970 with Rank Xerox in London, he was quickly headhunted by Grand Metropolitan Hotels and then became a Money Broker in the City. He joined Reuters, the international news and financial information leader in the early 1980s and became a main Board Director for their Transaction Services in 1990, moving to New York in 1994 to take control of their major accounts strategy for US banks. Reuters' International sales to these banks grew rapidly and as a result, Bob was appointed to organize professional sales training for the entire company.

In 2000, Bob left Reuters and set about expanding SpokenWord Ltd., a London-based sales training business he had already established with his business partner, Frances Tipper.

Today, he leads sales and negotiation programs for many international, high-profile clients and is in demand as an inspiring and charismatic speaker at business conferences around the world. He has also developed several successful US business interests.

People wishing to contact Bob can do so via SpokenWord's website www.spokenwordltd.com

ALSO BY BOB ETHERINGTON

Presentation Skills for Quivering Wrecks

10 reasons you must buy this book and avoid, "Death by slide-show"

1. Most business audiences have a single objective: to get out of the room.
2. Most business presenters have a single objective: to sit down in the audience again.
3. Most corporate audiences can't remember, 24 hours later, what was presented, the title of the presentation or the presenter's name.
4. Like it or not, 55% of the persuasive power of a presentation is transmitted by the speaker's body language; 38% by the speaker's voice tone and only 7% by the content.
5. 75% of speaker-nerves disappear with correct rehearsal.
6. You can discover how to generate applause when you want it.
7. There is a simple model you can use which will create a terrific presentation for you every time.
8. Bullet points are not what slides are for and using all capital letters makes text very hard to read.
9. Reading words off slides (as most presenters do) puts your audience to sleep in about 30 seconds.
10. Good Presenters are very rare. When you become a good presenter you can often negotiate better employment terms, higher salary, and even get yourself promoted (I did … so can you).

ISBN-13   978-904879-80-0
ISBN-10   1-904879-80-2

UK £8.99/USA $16.95/CAN $22.95